*Clamor Schürmann's
Barngarla grammar*

This book is available as a free fully-searchable ebook from
www.adelaide.edu.au/press

Clamor Schürmann's Barngarla grammar

A commentary on the first section of
A vocabulary of the Parnkalla language

(revised edition 2018)

by

Mark Clendon

Linguistics Department, Faculty of Arts
The University of Adelaide

UNIVERSITY OF
ADELAIDE PRESS

Clamor Wilhelm Schürmann

Published in Adelaide by

University of Adelaide Press
The University of Adelaide
Level 14, 115 Grenfell Street
South Australia 5005
press@adelaide.edu.au
www.adelaide.edu.au/press

The University of Adelaide Press publishes externally refereed scholarly books by staff of the University of Adelaide. It aims to maximise access to the University's best research by publishing works through the internet as free downloads and for sale as high quality printed volumes.

© 2015 Mark Clendon, 2018 for this revised edition

This work is licenced under the Creative Commons Attribution-NonCommercial-NoDerivatives 4.0 International (CC BY-NC-ND 4.0) License. To view a copy of this licence, visit http://creativecommons.org/licenses/by-nc-nd/4.0 or send a letter to Creative Commons, 444 Castro Street, Suite 900, Mountain View, California, 94041, USA. This licence allows for the copying, distribution, display and performance of this work for non-commercial purposes providing the work is clearly attributed to the copyright holders. Address all inquiries to the Director at the above address.

For the full Cataloguing-in-Publication data please contact the National Library of Australia: cip@nla.gov.au

ISBN (paperback) 978-1-925261-10-3
ISBN (ebook: pdf) 978-1-925261-11-0
ISBN (ebook: epub) 978-1-925261-12-7
ISBN (ebook: kindle) 978-1-925261-13-4

Project coordinator: Julia Keller
Book design: Zoë Stokes
Cover design: Emma Spoehr
Cover image: George French Angas, Australia, 1822-1886, *Port Lincoln from Winter's Hill*, 1845, Adelaide, watercolour on paper, 24.6 x 34.1 cm, Bequest of J Angas Johnson 1902, Art Gallery of South Australia, Adelaide, 0.621
Paperback printed by Griffin Press, South Australia

Contents

Frontispiece: Clamor Wilhelm Schürmann — v
Abbreviations used in glossing sentence examples & in the text — xi
Preface — xiii
Map: The northern and western Thura-Yura languages — xv

1 **Introduction** — 1
   1.1 Barngarla in geographical context
   1.2 Clamor Schürmann
   1.3 Barngarla documentation
   1.4 Procedure

2 **Writing Barngarla sounds** — 13
   2.1 Consonants
   2.2 Rhotics
   2.3 Vowels
   2.4 Sandhi

3 **Pronouns** — 22
   3.1 Pronoun forms
   3.2 Case alignment

4 **Intransitive verbs** — 37
   4.1 Introduction
   4.2 Present-tense verbs
   4.3 Pronoun suffixes
   4.4 Other tenses, aspects & moods

Clamor Schürmann's Barngarla grammar

5 Transitive verbs — 56
- 5.1 Present tense
- 5.2 The 3 sg ergative short-form pronoun
- 5.3 Past tense
- 5.4 Imperative
- 5.5 Hortative
- 5.6 Desiderative
- 5.7 Perfect aspect
- 5.8 Subjunctive present
- 5.9 Subjunctive past
- 5.10 Pluperfect

6 Harry Crawford's Barngarla verbs — 68

7 Suffixes on nouns — 71
- 7.1 Markedness
- 7.2 Plural & dual
- 7.3 Ergative & locative
- 7.4 Possessive, allative & purposive
- 7.5 Other grammatical suffixes

8 Other suffixes — 95
- 8.1 Grammatical endings
- 8.2 Discourse-pragmatic markers
- 8.3 Derivational/relativising

9 Demonstrative & interrogative pronouns — 111
- 9.1 This and that
- 9.2 Here and there
- 9.3 Who? What?
- 9.4 Which? Where? How?

10	**Verbal derivational affixes**	117
	10.1 Continuous derivation	
	10.2 Intransitive verbalisers with stative meaning	
	10.3 Inchoative	
	10.4 Reflexive & reciprocal verbs	
	10.5 Middle verbs	
	10.6 Present participles	
	10.7 Causative	
	10.8 Benefactive & applicative	
11	**Non-finite verbs**	153
	11.1 Infinitives	
	11.2 Gerunds	
	11.3 Other forms	
12	**Putting words together**	163
	12.1 Using pronouns	
	12.2 Verbless sentences	
	12.3 Existential verbs	
	12.3 Existential verbs	
	12.4 Body-part nouns	
	12.5 Complex predication	
	12.6 Negation	
13	**Prospect**	176
	Appendix: The name *Barngarla*	179
	References	183

Abbreviations used in glossing sentence examples & in the text

1	first person	LOC	locative case
2	second person	MATR	matrilineal pronoun
2,3	second & third person	NEG	negator
3	third person	NOM	nominative/absolutive case
ABL	ablative case	PAST	past tense
ALL	allative case	PATR	patrilineal pronoun
APPL	applicative verbaliser	PERF	perfect aspect
ASSOC	associative	PERL	perlative case
COM	comitative case	pl, PL	plural
CONJ	conjunction	POSS	possessive case
CONT	continuous aspect	PPL	participial affix
DAT	dative case	PRES	present tense
DIR	directional	PURP	purposive marker
du, DU	dual	RECIP	reciprocal affix
EMPH	emphatic	REDUP	reduplicated segment
EP	epenthetic morph	REL	relativising
EPIST	epistemic	RFLX	reflexive/reciprocal affix
ERG	ergative case	sg	singular
GER	gerund	SJTV	subjunctive mood
HUM.PL	human plural marker	TOP	topic
IMP	imperative mood	V	any unspecified vowel
INCH	inchoative	VBLZR	verbaliser
INF	infinitive	VOC	vocative case
INST	instrumental case	*x	unattested form
INTER	interrogative marker	x*	reconstructed form
INTR	intransitive		

Preface

This commentary on the grammatical introduction to Pastor Clamor Schürmann's *Vocabulary of the Parnkalla language* of 1844 is designed primarily for educators and other people who may wish to re-present its interpretations in ways more accessible to non-linguists, and more suited to pedagogical practice. It should be seen as one of a number of starting-points for language-reclamation endeavours in Barngarla, and is framed as a component in a Barngarla reclamation project undertaken by the University of Adelaide, and supported by the Commonwealth of Australia.[1]

Grammar is the acoustic-auditory code we use to signal. Language has evolved over the last 1.5 million years at least, and our signals are infinitely varied and extraordinarily complex.[2] Grammar, therefore, could be likened to a mathematical geometry of human cognition. This means that grammar is complex, and Australian languages are as complex as any. Being complex signalling systems, with emotion and culture overlying their geometry, no language is inherently easy for adults to learn; nor is it possible to describe them simply in any interesting detail. While I have tried to make this commentary accessible, it inevitably includes material that is more involved than many non-linguists will wish to take on board at a first reading. It has not been my intention to avoid or skim over difficult or unfamiliar areas of Barngarla grammar, for to do so would be to show scant respect both to Schürmann and to the language itself.

I am indebted to Jane Simpson of the Australian National University for providing me with a copy of Schürmann's vocabulary in an electronic file. This searchable version of the Barngarla vocabulary enabled a more comprehensive appreciation of the language than would have been otherwise achieved. And I am

---

[1] Grant no. 1001592-1000002338: *Online Learning Space: Barngarla Language.* Awarded under the Indigenous Languages Support-New Media initiative within the Attorney General's Department of the Ministry for the Arts; Ghil'ad Zuckermann Chief Investigator.

[2] On the antiquity of language see Dediu & Levinson (2013).

most especially indebted to Luise Hercus for making available her notes on Kuyani, recorded from the last full speaker of that language, and which constitute the most thorough modern documentation we have of any Thura-Yura language.

Mark Clendon
Adelaide, July 2015

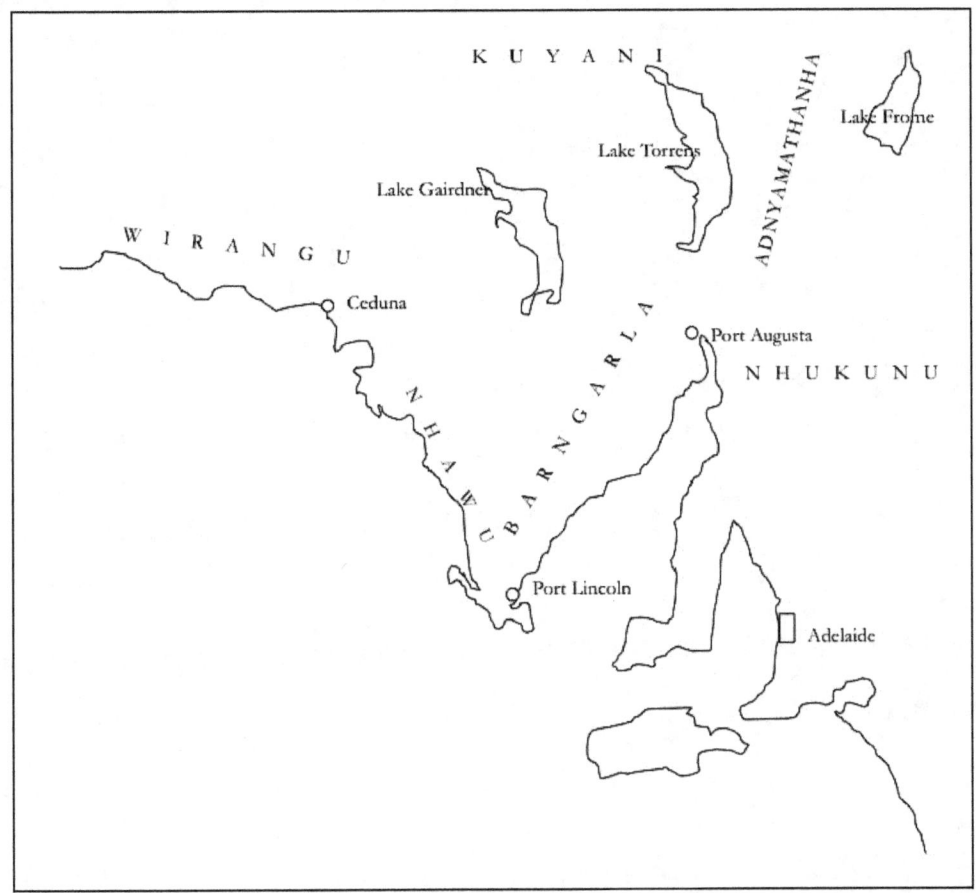

The northern and western Thura-Yura languages

One: Introduction

This commentary will seek to recast the first twenty-two pages of Clamor Schürmann's 1844 *Vocabulary of the Parnkalla language* in the light of contemporary understandings about other Thura-Yura languages, and about Australian languages more generally.

We are unusually fortunate in having a nineteenth-century grammar and vocabulary of Barngarla of such a high standard. Not only was the Lutheran pastor and missionary Clamor Schürmann an intelligent and accomplished linguist, but as a native speaker of German he was unhindered by the etymologically transparent but transcriptionally disastrous conventions of English spelling. The work of the German Lutheran missionaries on South Australian languages in the first half of the nineteenth century has few contemporary parallels for thoroughness and clarity. We are, therefore, and comparatively speaking, in an excellent position to reconstruct a good deal of Barngarla's phonology and morphology, and some of its syntax.

1.1 Barngarla in geographical context

Barngarla is a member of South Australia's Thura-Yura group of languages, one which was spoken traditionally on the Eyre Peninsula and north into the Gawler Rangers as far as the southern end of Lake Torrens, but probably not along the peninsula's west coast. An historical survey of the Thura-Yura group is presented in Simpson & Hercus (2004), along with a review of features that distinguish these languages from others around them, as well as those features that unite them as a group; and with argumentation for an ultimate phylogenetic origin.

Thura-Yura languages historically constituted a dialect spread from the Mount Lofty Ranges in the southeast, up to the northern Flinders Ranges in the north, and across to South Australia's west coast. We know, for example, that the southern languages Kaurna, Nhukunu and Nharangga were mutually intelligible; that Adnyamathanha, Kuyani and Barngarla were mutually intelligible, at least near their margins; and that it is likely that Nhawu, Barngarla and Wirangu were also mutually intelligible, again near their margins at least. About Ngadjuri we have almost no information at all. This kind of linguistic geography is observable in many parts of the world, and is characteristic of small-scale traditionally-oriented societies which have shared social institutions, and in the absence of major geographical barriers.

Thura-Yura languages share a number of features — both phonological and morphological — which collectively serve to distinguish them from surrounding languages. A full inventory of these is presented in Simpson & Hercus (2004), while only a summary of their most noticeable features will be attempted here.

At the level of phonology, Thura-Yura languages show a three-way rhotic contrast (a trill, a flap and a retroflex glide). The pronunciation of nasal and lateral consonants in many words may be made with a stop consonant at the same place of articulation inserted in front of them (prestopping). As an example of this, note the Barngarla verb root meaning 'fall,' *warni-*, compared to the same root in Kuyani, pronounced with a prestopped nasal, as *wardni-*, and the very common Australian 1st person dual pronoun *ngali* 'we two' pronounced in Barngarla with a prestopped lateral as *ngadli*.

Dative case-marking suffixes *-Ru* and *-ni* are employed in most Thura-Yura languages, and a verbal present continuous tense-ending *-ntha,* or variations thereupon, is also common to most Thura-Yura languages. A stop consonant may be omitted from sonorant-stop clusters: so where Kuyani and Kaurna have *-ngku* and *-ngka* as ergative and locative case suffixes respectively, Barngarla and Adnyamathanha have *-nga* for both these meanings.[1] The Barngarla, Kuyani and Adnyamathanha verbal applicative suffix is found as both *-ngku-* and *-ngu-*; and the

---

[1] Barngarla also shows *-ngi* and *-ngu*.

Kuyani verb root *karlda-* 'call out' appears in Barngarla as *garla* 'call out.' The Wirangu words *ngaldi* 'liver' and *bindhara* 'salt lake' are found in southern Barngarla as *ngali* and *binhara* respectively. Finally, many phonologically compounded words in Thura-Yura languages are formed by omitting the first consonant of the second word or morpheme. As an example of this, note the Barngarla relativizing suffix *-bidni* attached to the adverb *yarrgulu* 'before' to make the compound *yarrguludni* 'ancient': *yarrgulu* + *bidni* → *yarrguludni*.

Thura-Yura languages show correspondences between stop consonants that occur at the beginning of words. Words that start with the consonant *th/dh* in most other Thura-Yura languages, often start with *y* in Barngarla and Adnyamathanha. Words that start with *p/b* in other languages start with *v* in Adnyamathanha, and the consonant *k/g* is lost from the start of most Adnyamathanha words.

Societies speaking Thura-Yura languages possessed as well a number of distinctive cultural features, some of which they shared with people living in the Lake Eyre Basin. The brief summary attempted here follows that of Hercus (2006c).

Among practices shared with the Lake Eyre Basin was a kinship system divided between two exogamous moieties called (in the orthography that will be suggested here) *Madharhi* and *Garharru*, which Schürmann (1846/2009: 222) spelled *Mattiri* and *Karraru*. This system appears to have extended south and east as far as the country of people who spoke Nhukunu, but not to have included speakers of Ngadjuri or Kaurna. Linguistically, the moiety system was operated by way of an elaborate set of pronouns including up to ten series, one of which could be selected on any occasion to address or refer to different categories of kinfolk.[2] Schürmann recorded three or four of these series in Barngarla, although there are likely to have been more, which he may have missed. The three he recorded may be represented by 1st person dual forms: *ngadli*, *ngadlaga* and *ngarinyi;* but he did not record their references consistently, at pages 12-13 of his grammar, and on page 251 of his later work. The anomalies may be summarized as follows:

---

[2] See Hercus & White (1973) and Schebeck (1973) for the way this system operated in Adnyamathanha.

	ngadli	*ngadlaga*	*ngarinyi*	*budlanbi* (3rd dual)
Gramm: 12-13	—	matrilineal	patrilineal	affinal
Manners: 251	siblings	affinal	parent-child	—

In this commentary I will follow the explanation put forward in the grammar section of his vocabulary, as that appears to match more closely the Adnyamathanha system as described by Schebeck (1973) and Hercus & White (1973).

Thura-Yura languages also possess a system of nine birth-order names, with separate terms for male and female children.[3] This system is recorded for Kaurna in Amery & Simpson (2013: 15), and for Adnyamathanha in Schebeck (1973: 27). The birth-order names that Schürmann recorded for Barngarla are as follows:

	Female		Male	
	Schürmann	Phonemic	Schürmann	Phonemic
First born:	Kartanya	*Gardanya*	Piri	*Birhi*
Second born:	Warruyu[4]	*Warruyu*	Wari, Warri	*Warri*
Third born:	Kunta	*Gunda*	Kunni	*Guni*
Fourth born:	Munnaka	*Munaga*	Munni	*Muni*
Fifth born:	Marruko	*Marruga*	Marri	*Marri*
Sixth born:	Yarranta	*Yaranda*	Yarri	*Yara*
Seventh born:	Méllakka	*Milaga*	Milli	*Mili*
Eighth born:	Wanggurtu	*Wanggurdu*	Wangguyu	*Wangguyu*
Ninth born:	Ngallaka	*Ngarlaga*	Ngallai	*Ngarlayi*

The left-hand columns in each case record Schürmann's spelling, while the right-hand columns in italics suggest how these words may be represented phonemically, in the spelling system to be used in this commentary. Phonemic forms may be read primarily off the Adnyamathanha terms, and supported by the Kaurna

---

[3] This is a lexical gender system: a first-born child is *Kartanya* if a girl, or *Piri* if a boy; a second-born child is *Warruyu* if a girl, or *Warri* if a boy, and so on.

[4] Also *Wayuru*.

terms. Nhukunu and Kuyani have *pirtiya/pirdiya* for the first-born son (Hercus 1992: 27, 2006a), so we may guess that the Barngarla word also has a retroflex second consonant. Nhukunu has *milatu* and *miliya* for eighth-born daughters and sons respectively, and Kuyani has *milaka* for the eighth-born daughter (Hercus 1992: 23, 2006a). This makes it clear that the lateral in the Barngarla words was also alveolar.

The *Wilyaru* ritual was practised by people speaking the northern and western Thura-Yura languages Adnyamathanha, Barngarla, Wirangu and Kuyani. Hercus (2006c) contains a more detailed account of, as well as historical references to, this ritual. The *Wilyaru* was performed as well in the Lake Eyre Basin, and by Arrernte-speaking people in the north of South Australia. The *Wilyaru* was called in Barngarla *Wilyalginyi* (Schürmann 1846/2009: 231-234). This word appears to have been used to refer to both the ceremony itself and to the men who took part in it. It was in Barngarla society the third and final stage of male initiation, undertaken by young men of about eighteen, and involved the cutting of long parallel scars or cicatrices on the back. Adnyamathanha people maintained this ceremony up until the late 1930s.

Thura-Yura languages share lexical and grammatical features with languages to their north in the Lake Eyre Basin (eg Hercus 1999: 133), and further away, with languages in the southeast of the Northern Territory and with those on the Darling River. East of the Mount Lofty Ranges, however, along the lower reaches of the River Murray, the eastern Fleurieu Peninsula and the Coorong, Ngarrinyeric languages are spoken, in a number of varieties or dialects including Ramindjeri, Yaraldi, Ngarrindjeri and Tanganekald. These languages are significantly different in their grammars and lexica from the languages to their west and north: the Mount Lofty Range represents a major discontinuity in Australia's linguistic geography between Ngarrinyeric languages to the east, and Thura-Yura languages to the west and northwest.

The origins of this discontinuity may go back to the last ice-age. Under conditions of increased aridity and decreased temperature, the Lower River Murray may have provided then, as it must always have done, hospitable conditions in an otherwise fairly inhospitable environment. People are likely to have remained living along the Lower Murray in considerable numbers throughout the last glaciation, after other more arid landscapes had suffered possibly quite dramatic reductions in population. When at the onset of the holocene the vast southern plains of inland Australia were effectively re-colonized from the Dividing Range (Clendon 2006, McConvell & Alpher 2002), the languages of the Lower Murray may have by that time diverged significantly from other Pama-Nyungan languages.

A summary of what little is known about Barngarla dialectology is set out in Hercus (1999: 12-13). Barngarla-speakers were probably never very numerous, and were dispersed throughout a large and largely semi-arid region. Their speech would have differed in relatively minor ways from place to place: many of the differences would have been characteristic of particular extended families in particular places, and may not always have been reified or labelled. Hercus (1999: 12-13) discusses evidence for a northern variety of Barngarla having a number of frequently-used lexical items shared with Wirangu rather than with the Barngarla spoken around Port Lincoln.

West of Port Lincoln, around Coffin Bay and up along the coast north-westward from there, people spoke a Thura-Yura variety called Nhawu. Schürmann's Barngarla associates were clear that this name referred to a distinct group, but then they were also clear that other named groups were distinct: they referred to Badharra *(Eucalypt sp)* people, and Wambiri (coastal) people as well. Nevertheless Nhawu probably was in some respects noticeably different from Barngarla, as the following sentence example from Schürmann's vocabulary shows:

(1.1) (23)

1	SCHÜRMANN:	kurrirrurriri	Nauurri	wanggatanna
2	PHONEMIC:	guRiRuRiri	Nhawurri	wanggadhanha
3	MORPHEMES:	guRi-RuRi-ri	Nhawu-rri	wangga-dha-nha
4	GLOSS:	twist-REDUP-VBLZR	NAME-HUM.PL	speak-PRES-2,3.pl
5	TRANSLATION:	*the Nauos talk unintelligibly*		

Barngarla *kurrirrurriri* is 'round about,' and Kuyani has *kuRi-kuRi* 'go round and round' (Hercus 2006a) based on *kuRi-* 'bind up, twist.' Schürmann' translation 'unintelligibly' for *guRiRuRiri* is almost certainly an overstatement.

Only the first and fifth lines in the above sentence example are Schürmann's; the other lines have been introduced to show the sentence's phonemic representation in line 2, its morphology in line 3, and its morpheme glosses in line 4. All sentence examples taken from Schürmann's book will be in this form, with five lines as indicated, and with the page number where the example is to be found in his vocabulary appearing either above the sentence and after the sentence example number as here, or in the left-hand margin and below the example number. The grammar and vocabulary sections of Schürmann's book are paginated separately, so all sentence examples taken from the grammar section will have their page numbers prefixed with the letter *g*.

Very few words of Nhawu have survived, Schürmann's (1846/2009: 250) list of ten Nhawu words being all we have. Hercus (1999: 13-15) makes a case that Nhawu may have been closer to Wirangu than to Barngarla, and that it may also have been intermediary between both. Hercus & Simpson (2001) is a comprehensive account of all that we know about this Thura-Yura speech.

The only Thura-Yura language with remaining full speakers is Adnyamathanha. According to the website of the University of Adelaide's Mobile Language Team there are currently around twenty Adnyamathanha speakers in 2014, living in both the Flinders Ranges and in Adelaide.[5] Adnyamathanha was in a dialectal relationship with Kuyani, a Thura-Yura language spoken to the west and northwest of the Flinders Ranges, around the northern end of Lake Torrens. Luise Hercus recorded Kuyani spoken by Alice Oldfield, its last full speaker, in 1975 (Hercus 2006a-c). We have a sketch grammar of Wirangu (Hercus 1999), and a small dictionary of Nhukunu (Hercus 1992). The language of the Adelaide Plain, Kaurna, was well described by Christian Teichelmann and Clamor Schürmann in the nineteenth century (Teichelmann & Schürmann 1840), and has been undergoing reclamation and revival work since the 1990s (e.g. Amery 2016, Amery & Simpson 2013). However very little material survives of Nharangga or of Ngadjuri.

---

[5] Adnyamathanha is commonly referred to as *Yurha Ngawarla* 'human speech' by at least some of its speakers in the Flinders Ranges (Schebeck 1973: 24, Tunbridge 1996: 29).

1.2   Clamor Schürmann

Clamor Wilhelm Schürmann was born in 1815 in Schledehausen near Osnabrück, in Lower Saxony. In 1832 aged seventeen he travelled to Berlin to enter the Lutheran Seminary there, where he studied Latin, New Testament Greek, German Grammar, English and Hebrew. In 1836 aged twenty-one he entered the Seminary of the Lutheran Mission Society in Dresden, and in 1838 he travelled as a missionary to Adelaide in the new colony of South Australia, founded just two years previously.

He journeyed there with a fellow Lutheran student and missionary from Dresden, Christian Teichelmann. Three settlements of German colonists flourished in Adelaide from an early date: Klemzig on the plain, and Hahndorf and Lobethal in the hills east of the town; as well as settlements in the Barossa Valley some seventy kilometres northeast of Adelaide. Schürmann and Teichelmann were both intelligent and well-trained in languages, and both took a sound professional interest in the language they encountered on the Adelaide plain. Within two years they had produced their *Outlines of a grammar, vocabulary and phraseology of the Aboriginal language of South Australia*.

In 1840, the year this book was published, aged only twenty-five, Schürmann travelled to Port Lincoln on the southern tip of the Eyre Peninsula to act as missionary to, and Assistant Protector of Aboriginal people there. In 1844 Schürmann published his *Vocabulary of the Parnkalla language*, and in 1846 *The Aboriginal tribes of Port Lincoln*. Schürmann was based in Port Lincoln for 13 years until 1853, when he returned to Adelaide, and soon after travelled to undertake pastoral work in Western Victoria.

The next 40 years of his life were spent among Lutheran communities in Western Victoria and South Australia. He is recorded as being of small stature, ruddy complexion and of a particularly genial disposition. He was esteemed for his humility, kindness, straightforwardness and conscientious devotion to duty (Schurmann 1987: 207). He died in Bethany, in South Australia's Barossa Valley in 1893, aged 78, and is buried in Hamilton, Victoria.

A comprehensive account of Schürmann's life and work in South Australia and Victoria may be found in Schurmann (1987), a biography written by his great-grandson.

1.3   Barngarla documentation

The copy of the vocabulary from which I have been working includes pages with typed notes added to the original published edition at some later date. Near the front of the copy beneath the stamp of the South Australian Museum are three or four handwritten notes as follows:

(1)   With additions by C W Schürmann from his ms notes.
(2)   (annotated about   )
(3)   Received from the Public Library. This copy was bound and given to the S. a. Museum as return for the gift to them of Schürmann's own copy with his manuscript additions. There are additional annotations by N B Tindale.
(4)   N B Tindale compared this copy line for line with the above Schürmann annotated copy on June 6 1972

Beneath the first note, very faintly, is a note that appears to read 'annotated about ___' with what may have been a date, now illegible.

On the face of it therefore, the authorship of the additions could be problematic. Nevertheless typewriters were commercially produced after 1873, and the spelling of Barngarla words used in the added typewritten notes is the same as that used by Schürmann in the original edition. It is certain, then, that these notes are by Schürmann rather than by Tindale, compiled from his earlier notebooks. Tindale's own notes are handwritten, and usually initialled.

Tindale himself, around about 1934, transferred Schürmann's vocabulary onto a set of index cards, now held in the South Australian Museum archives (Tindale 1934a, b). The record entry for these items includes the descriptor 'C W Schürmann 1884,' so this is likely to be the year in which he annotated an original copy of his vocabulary.

Over 250 kilometers to the northeast of Port Lincoln, the American linguist Ken Hale recorded Barngarla man Harry Crawford, also called Harry Croft, at Iron Knob 'through a doorway of a house' one day in 1960 (O'Grady 2001). By that time there were apparently only three Barngarla speakers remaining, and Crawford's language is clearly influenced by Wirangu and Kukarta. Of the 380 items in Hale's vocabulary questionnaire, Crawford was able to respond to seventy-eight (20%), so it is likely that he had not used Barngarla regularly for many years. Nevertheless his record offers us a valuable perspective and check on the language Schürmann recorded over a hundred years earlier.

In 1965 and 1966 at Point Pearce and Andamooka Luise Hercus recorded Moonie Davis speaking Barngarla, in lists of vocabulary items and in elicited sentences. Davis' main language was Kukarta, but he was apparently proficient as well in Barngarla (Hercus 2006c). These recordings are held in Canberra at AIATSIS (Hercus 1965, 1966), and have recently formed the foundation of efforts to revive Barngarla on the Eyre Peninsula.[6]

Jane Simpson included analysis of some Barngarla morphology in a publication on historical language sources (Simpson 1995), and Luise Hercus' (1999) description of Wirangu contains a valuable discussion what is known of Barngarla dialectology, and of the relationships, apparently close, between Barngarla, Wirangu and Nhawu on the Eyre Peninsula.

A more extensive bibliography of archival material relating to Barngarla may be found on the website of the University of Adelaide's Mobile Language Team.[7]

1.4 Procedure

Phonemic representations of the words presented in Schürmann's 1844 grammar and vocabulary may be attempted by comparing his work with that of authors writing in the middle and late twentieth century, about the then currently spoken Thura-Yura languages Adnyamathanha, Wirangu, Kuyani and Nhukunu. Tun-

---

[6] http://www.mobilelanguageteam.com.au/about/detail/mlt_cadet_dawn_taylor_wakes_up_the_barngarla_language1 (accessed 4/11/14).

[7] http://www.mobilelanguageteam.com.au/languages/resources/barngarla

bridge (1988: 281, fn 5) claims that Barngarla and Adnyamathanha were in a dialectal relationship, and that Adnyamathana speakers confirmed that these two languages were mutually intelligible. Nevertheless Barngarla was spoken over a wide area, and would have almost certainly shown regional differences. It is worth remembering that the language Schürmann recorded was spoken around Port Lincoln, roughly 300 to 400 kilometres southwest of the southern Flinders Ranges. The reconstruction of the Adelaide language currently referred to as Kaurna (Amery & Simpson 2013) may also be used cautiously for this purpose. Kuyani and Nhukunu have ceased to be spoken since recordings were made in the 1970s (Hercus 1992, 2006).

The comparison undertaken here proceeds on the understanding that twentieth-century authors have benefited from our increased knowledge of Australian languages and of contemporary linguistic practice over the 130 or so years since Schürmann wrote his Barngarla grammar and vocabulary. And although this is certainly the case, it would nevertheless be a mistake to imagine that recent transcriptions of living Thura-Yura languages are unproblematic. None but fairly cursory accounts of the phonology of any Thura-Yura language exist, and phonemic representations are sometimes inconsistent, even within the work of a single author.

Where I have been able to find correspondences in contemporary or recently-spoken and recorded Thura-Yura languages, or in Kaurna, for the Barngarla words and suffixes Schürmann transcribed, I will note those correspondences; where I have been unable to find correspondences I will adhere to Schürmann's spelling, exception being made where his representation contradicts what we know about Thura-Yura phonology generally, and about Barngarla phonology and morphology in particular.

Schürmann published his Barngarla vocabulary after four years in Port Lincoln. He was to spend another nine years there, during which time he clearly discovered more about the language than he had put into the vocabulary. Unfortunately many of the sentence examples added after the book was published lack translations, and this occasions some difficulty with respect to recognizing grammatical phenomena.

This commentary by no means exhausts all that could be discovered about Barngarla from Schürmann's vocabulary. A full review of the vocabulary section would almost certainly reveal more insights about the way Barngarla was used, which in turn could add to and modify the grammar he presents in its first twenty-two pages.

Two: Writing Barngarla sounds

2.1 Consonants

From a comparison of Schürmann's material with the phoneme inventories of Adnyamathanha (Tunstill 2004: 459), Nhukunu (Hercus 1992: 3), Wirangu (Hercus 1999: 26) and Kaurna (Amery & Simpson 2013: 29), Barngarla seems to have had a normal Australian consonant inventory. We are able to reconstruct unvoiced, unaspirated stops at six places of articulation, including two laminal series — lamino-dental and lamino-palatal — and two apical series, apico-alveolar and apico-postalveolar (or retroflex) — orthographically represented by the voiced grapheme series. There are also six matching nasals and four matching laterals at coronal points of articulation, as shown below:

	bilabial	dental	alveolar	retroflex	palatal	velar
stops:	b	dh	d	rd	dy	g
nasals:	m	nh	n	rn	ny	ng
laterals:		lh	l	rl	ly	
rhotic trill:			rr			
rhotic tap:			r			
glides:	w			rh/R	y	

As well, all nasal and lateral sounds that are not velar can be prestopped when they occur at the start of the second syllable in a word. That is, they can be pronounced with a stop consonant at the same place of articulation in front of them. The relevant nasal and lateral sounds are shaded in the above chart. The prestopped nasal and lateral phonemes are shown below:

	bilabial	dental	alveolar	retroflex	palatal
prestopped nasals:	bm	dnh	dn	rdn	dny
prestopped laterals:		dlh	dl	rdl	dly

Prestopping appears to have been to some extent optional in the area around Port Lincoln where Schürmann worked.

Words seem not to have been able to begin with apical consonants; instead laminal consonants, as well as bilabial and velar consonants, occur in this position (Simpson & Hercus 2004: 186-188). Lamino-dental consonants occur at the start of words before *a* and *u* (eg *dha-, dhu-),* and lamino-palatal consonants occur at the start of words before *i (dyi-).* Words can start with a vowel, and all words must end with a vowel.

There is one example in Schürmann's vocabulary of the three-consonant cluster *nky*, in the verb *pinkyata/ binkyadha* 'call, name.' This cluster occurs also in Kaurna, but rarely, along with the cluster *ngky*.

2.1.1 Vowel fronting

The German missionaries recorded the phonetic raising and fronting of the vowels *a* and *u* before lamino-palatal consonants by the digraphs ⟨ai⟩ and ⟨ui⟩, and by the letter ⟨ü⟩: examples are *paitya* for phonemic-orthographic *badya* 'angry,' *wailbi* for phonemic *walybi* 'southwest,' *ngukaintya* for phonemic *nguganydya* 'have gone,' *murtuitya* for phonemic *murdudya* 'different, separate,' *tuin-nga* for phonemic *dhunynga*, (without a gloss), *partütyuru* for phonemic *bardudyuru* 'long rumped,' *murtünyu* for phonemic *murdunyu* 'species of fish,' and *kauülyaranna* for phonemic *gawulyaranha* 'lots of water.' This is quite consistent, and usually indicates the lamino-palatal position of a following consonant. Schürmann also seems to have regularly, although by no means infallibly, recorded the lamino-dental nasal *nh* as orthographic *nn* in his text, and the retroflex lateral *rl* as *ll*.

2.2 Rhotics

There is likely to have been a three-way rhotic contrast in Barngarla, as is the case in other Thura-Yura languages (Simpson & Hercus 2004: 185), although as Hercus (1999: 33) notes: 'in Thura-Yura the trilled *rr* is not a particularly frequent phoneme.' For Barngarla this contrast is unlikely to be recoverable in full or with certainty from historical texts. At Iron Knob Harry Crawford attested only two rhotics, a glide and apparently a trill, but Crawford's speech was influenced by Wirangu, which has only these two, and he does not appear to have been using Barngarla regularly at the time Ken Hale interviewed him (O'Grady 2001). The way Thura-Yura rhotics have been represented in spelling over the years is nothing if not luxuriant:

PHONEME	SPELLING	AUTHORS	KEY:
Apico-alveolar trill:	rr	1, 2, 3, 5, 6	1 *Amery & Simpson*
	ř	7	2 *Hercus*
Apico-alveolar flap:	r	2, 3, 4, 7	3 *McEntee & McKenzie*
	rh	5	4 *Miller et al*
	rd	1	5 *O'Grady et al*
	d	6	6 *SA Education Dept*
Retroflex glide:	r	3, 7	7 *Schebeck*
	R	2, 4	8 *Warlpiri*
	r	1, 5, 6	
Retroflex flap:	d	7	
	đ	3	
	rd	6, 8	

The retroflex flap is apparently found only in Adnyamathanha, and in Warlpiri in the Northern Territory.

2.2.1 A fourth rhotic

Adnyamathanha appears to have a four-way rhotic contrast (Schebeck 1974: xvi, McEntee & McKenzie 1992: ix, Tunbridge 1996: 31), although this may be the case at a phonetic level only. Tunbridge (1996: 31) notes that Adnyamathanha's two rhotic flaps, apico-alveolar and apico-postalveolar (retroflex) respectively, are flapped between vowels, but are pronounced as stops elsewhere. Unless there is an intervocalic contrast between rhotics and stops at these places of articulation, they may represent single phonemes with flapped and stopped allophones. See also Simpson & Hercus (2004: 185, fn 7) for a diachronic perspective.

2.2.2 Barngarla rhotics

Schürmann identified three rhotics in Barngarla, and gives examples of the difference between two of them with three minimal pairs. He says 'the words in the right column have the peculiar sound [probably a trill] described above:'

yurra	*man*	yurra	*earth*
wirra	*scrub*	wirra	*air or rain*
karra	*high*	karra	*grass*

When we look for correspondences for these six words in contemporary transcriptions of other Thura-Yura languages we find the following, using the rhotic symbols (r, R, rr) used by Luise Hercus among others:

Words with a flap or tap (r):	Wirangu	wira	*sky*
Words with a retroflex glide (R):	Adnyamathanha	yuRa	*person*
	Kuyani	thuRa	*person*
	Wirangu	gaRa	*grass*
	Iron-Knob Barngarla	wiRa	*cloud*[8]
Words with a trill (rr):	Adnyamathanha	yurra	*dirt, earth*
	Kuyani	karra	*high*
	Adnyamathanha	arra	*high*
	Nhukunu	wirra	*scrub*

---

[8] Hale's transcription of Harry Crawford's word (see Chapter Six).

This gives us a completely different set of rhotic contrasts from the one Schürmann offers:

GLIDE (R)		TRILL (rr)		TAP (r)	
yuRa	*man, person*	yurra	dirt, earth		
kaRa	*grass*	karra	*high*		
wiRa	*cloud*	wirra	*scrub*	wira	*sky*

Schürmann's *wirra* is 'air or rain,' Wirangu *wira* is 'sky' and Harry Crawford's *wiRa* is 'cloud' — three different transcriptions with three different attested meanings. Nevertheless it is probably the case that they represent a single word, with the unusual property that a flap in Wirangu appears to correspond to a glide in Iron Knob Barngarla. Because of my uncertainty as to which should be preferred, I have listed them both here.

The members of Schürmann's two columns are represented in all three rhotic categories, when compared to contemporary spoken languages. This could mean that Barngarla rhotics, while not corresponding to rhotics in other Thura-Yura languages, yet retained acoustic and articulatory coherence as a set of rhotics: but this is a rather unlikely situation. Perhaps more likely, is the possibility that while Schürmann recognized a rhotic contrast, he did not record it systematically, and did not recognize its significance. For this he cannot be blamed; for although trained in New Testament Greek, Latin and Biblical Hebrew, and fluent in German and English, none of these languages make any phonemic rhotic distinctions.

The third rhotic Schürmann distinguishes is not a rhotic at all; rather it is a clear perception of the articulatory qualities of retroflex consonants in Barngarla:

    yurne *or* yurdne   *throat*

Here we see a quite common phenomenon in Thura-Yura languages, in which nasal and lateral consonants may be optionally pre-stopped: in the first of these two words we see a retroflex nasal *rn*, and then the same sound prestopped as *rdn (=rdrn)*. These words correspond to their counterparts in other Thura-Yura languages, where they may also contain prestopped nasals:

Adnyamathanha, Nhukunu, Kuyani: *yurdni*
Kaurna: *yurni*
Barngarla: *yurdni, yurni*

2.2.3 Spelling rhotics

In order for Barngarla to be easily compared with other northern Thura-Yura languages, and in order for written material in those languages to be read consistently, it would seem reasonable for the representation of Barngarla rhotics to conform to the spelling conventions most commonly found in material about other Thura-Yura languages. The apico-alveolar trill is in Australia almost universally written *rr*, and for the apico-alveolar tap or flap most writers on Thura-Yura languages have used *r*. Most of the contemporary material on the northern languages has been written by Luise Hercus, who consistently uses *rr* for the trill and *r* for the flap or tap. It would therefore seem advantageous to maintain the use of these signs in Barngarla spelling. However for the retroflex glide, both diacritic *ṛ* and capitalized R could be inconvenient. The digraph *rh* might be used here, to capture the softness of this sound. With the foregoing in mind, the following conventions for Barngarla rhotics will be suggested in this commentary:

The rhotic trill: *rr*
The rhotic flap or tap: *r*
The retroflex glide: *rh*

2.3 Vowels

Like other northern Thura-Yura languages, Barngarla probably had four phonemic vowels: *a, i, u,* and long *aa* or *ā*. Schürmann, however, uses *e* and *o* as well. Vowel sounds represented in the spelling of early nineteenth-century German linguists are discussed by Amery & Simpson (2013: 32). Schürmann's *e* is phonemic *i*, and his *o* is phonemic *u*, with the following exceptions: his *e* is usually *a* after *y*, and his *o* is usually *a* after *w*.

Vowel harmony across morpheme boundaries is pervasive in Barngarla, although it may be sporadic. Vowels in a number of suffixes may optionally or obligatorily harmonize with their host nouns, and these will be noted as they occur.

The historical-orthographic observation that Schürmann's *o* is phonemic *a* after *w* does not apply at the ends of words. A number of examples may be adduced to support this contention, including one to be discussed in Section 4.2.4:

(i) Schürmann (1973: 125) lists *nauo, nawo* as the name of a language ('national name of the native tribe') spoken around Coffin Bay. This name can be shown to be phonemic *Nhawu*, with Schürmann's *o* representing phonemic *u* word-finally. In his grammar, but not his dictionary, Schürmann has the word *Nauurri* 'the Nauos,' referring to a group. This is *Nauu (Nhawu)* with the human plural suffix *-rri* on the end. Hercus & Simpson (2001: 284, 287) list early transcriptions of *Nauo*, which all point to a final *u*-sound; the only exception being the contemporary pronunciation of a senior Wangkangurru man who said *Nyaawa*, but this some 50 years after he had heard the word from Barngarla speakers. (ii) Schürmann (1973: 53) lists *kauo* 'water,' and Harry Crawford gives two words for 'water,' *kawi* and *kawu* (O'Grady 2001). This guarantees that Schürmann's word-final *o* is phonemic *u* in this word. (iii) On the same page Schürmann lists *kauokauurriti* (probably phonemic *gawu-gawuridhi*) 'to swing to and fro, being suspended.' This clearly shows a reduplicated root iconic of the repeated motion of its denotation. The second part of the root *(kauu/gawu)* reveals more clearly the phonemic representation of the first part, which Schürmann spells *kauo*. The upshot of this is that although Schürmann's *o* is usually phonemic *a* after *w*, this is not the case when these two sounds occur together in that order word-finally: in this position it is likely that his *-wo, -o* or *-uo* represent phonemic *-wu*.

2.4 Sandhi

Morphological sandhi processes undoubtedly affected vowels at morpheme boundaries, although observations on this important area of Thura-Yura phonology are few and indirect. Barngarla phonotactics probably did not allow vowel clusters or diphthongs. Although Schürmann's grammar and vocabulary are replete with orthographic vowel clusters such as *kaya ilka* [spear ASSOC] and *kulaka-itye* 'cut for me,' upon investigation these can usually be shown to involve anticipatory fronting and raising (see above), or the excrescence of a glide.

2.4.1 Vowel clusters

Accounts of Thura-Yura languages commonly imply that vowel clusters are part of Thura-Yura phonotactics, but there is evidence that such claims describe morphology, not phonology. Bernhard Schebeck's work in particular appears seldom to distinguish the two levels of description: for example his *marra-anha* 'fourth-born male child' (1973: 27, 42) is spelled *marr-anha* by McEntee & McKenzie (1992: 81) (among many other instances). Although concerned with justifying spelling, the discussion of Adnyamathanha sounds in Tunstill (2004: 464-466) points indirectly to an absence of phonemic vowel clusters in that language.

There appear to be at least two strategies available to deal with vowels brought into contact by morphological processes. Tunbridge (1996: 31) writing about Adnyamathanha states that 'when any two short vowels occur together in a word they generally come to be pronounced as a single long vowel with the phonetic value of the second of the two.' Evidence for the second part of this statement at least is available from Kuyani, where Hercus (2006c) notes the word *kuty'-alpila* 'the other two,' composed of *kutyu* 'other' and the dual suffix *-al(y)pila*. Here the final vowel of *kutyu* is elided, while the first vowel of the dual suffix remains; it does not lengthen, however. When considering in Section 4.3 the way in which enclitic pronouns are attached to Barngarla verbs, we will see that two short vowels need not make a long.

Kuyani evinces a second and competing phonological process, as seen in *kutyualpilangku* |kutyu-alpila-ngku| [other-DUAL-ERG] 'the other two (ergative)' (Hercus 2006c). Again, two vowels are brought together in this word, but this time without elision of either vowel. Hercus notes that the dual suffix is *-(w)alpila* after *u*, citing the word *paaRuwalpila* |paaRu-w-alpila| [meat-EP-DUAL] 'two sorts of meat' (2006c), with a glide excreted between the last vowel of *paaRu* and the first of *-alpila*: this is almost certainly the case with Hercus' *kutyualpilangku* as well.

Further investigation of a living Thura-Yura language will be required to discover what constraints, if any, apply to the application of these two phonological processes.

Three: Pronouns

3.1 Pronoun forms

In this section we will look at the different kinds of meaning that Barngarla pronouns code, and in the following section we will look at the kinds of grammatical functions coded on pronouns.

3.1.1 1st Singular

The first person singular pronoun (I, me) is shown below, with technical labels for its various meanings:

SCHÜRMANN	PHONEMIC	ENGLISH
First person singular		
ngai	ngayi	*I, me;* NOMINATIVE
ngatto	ngadhu	*I;* ERGATIVE
ngaitye	ngadyi	*of me, my, mine;* POSSESSIVE
ngaityidni	ngadyidni	*of or from me;* ABLATIVE
ngaityidninge	ngadyidningi	*with me;* COMITATIVE
ngaityidniru	ngadyidnirhu	*towards me;* ALLATIVE

Schürmann recognized two core cases in Barngarla, which he called *nominative* and *active nominative*. An understanding of these terms requires an understanding of the difference between intransitive and transitive verbs, which is explained again briefly in Section 4.1.2. He recognized a third case, *possessive*, but he did not provide labels for the other forms: the labels seen here are those commonly used in modern grammatical description.

The nominative case is the case of subjects of intransitive verbs, such as *she* in *she's sleeping*. The active nominative, or what is now called *ergative*, is the case of subjects of *transitive* verbs, such as *she* in *she saw me*. English does not have an ergative case, so in English the subjects of both transitive and intransitive verbs are the same. There is a third core case, called *accusative*, which is the case of *objects* of transitive verbs, such as *her* in *I saw her*. In Barngarla the subjects of intransitive verbs, and the objects of transitive verbs are treated in the same way, and this is what the term *nominative* refers to in Schürmann's grammar. A term *absolutive* may also be used to refer to the marking of subjects of intransitive verbs and objects of transitive verbs together, but I will stick with Schürmann's term *nominative* for this situation in this commentary. And so the core cases that are marked in Barngarla grammar are NOMINATIVE, covering intransitive subjects and transitive objects; and active-nominative or ERGATIVE, covered transitive subjects.

The possessive shape, like the possessive shape of all Barngarla pronouns, is used to signal ownership, but it is also used for other things. As you can see, it is used as a base or stem for the other cases, and this will be discussed in more detail in Section 3.2. Possessive shapes are used as well to mark someone who benefits from something: you may see an example of this use in sentence example (4.4) in Section 4.3.

An important case not represented in Schürmann's lists is DATIVE. This is the case that marks a human object of verbs that mean *give*: the person who is given, or who receives something. Barngarla nouns take a dative-case ending *-ni* (see Section 7.5.1), and dative pronouns take this same suffix: unusually it is attached to the *nominative*-case shape of the pronoun. So the dative-case shape of the 1st singular pronoun is *ngayini:* you may see an example of this in use in sentence example (4.4) in Section 7.5.1.

Barngarla has two ablative case suffixes: *-bidni* and *-ngurni* (for discussion see Sections 7.5.2 and 8.3.1). On pronouns these suffixes are shortened to *-idni* and *-urni*. Most pronouns use *-idni*, while three (2nd singular general, 2nd singular patrilineal and the interrogative pronoun *nganha*) use *-urni*, and two (1st singular and 1st pl) appear to be able to choose between these endings. The alternative ablative, comitative and allative shapes for the 1st singular pronoun are:

ngaityurni	ngadyurni	*of or from me;* ABLATIVE
ngaityurninge	ngadyurningi	*with me;* COMITATIVE
ngaityurniru	ngadyurnirhu	*towards me;* ALLATIVE

How the ergative shapes of pronouns and nouns are used will be discussed in Section 4.1.2.

The forms *ngayi* and *ngadhu* are amply attested in Adnyamathanha, Wirangu and Kuyani. Hercus (1999: 72) lists a set of Wirangu 1st singular possessive pronoun alternatives that fairly clearly include Barngarla *ngadyi*. The form *ngadyidnirhu* probably contains the common Thura-Yura genitive/allative suffix *-rhu*, with a retroflex rhotic (cf Schebeck 1974: 6-7, Hercus 2006a), and so this suffix is represented in this way here and in the paradigms that follow.

3.1.2 Pronoun series

Nearly all the languages starting from the southeast of the Northern Territory and extending down around Lake Eyre and through the centre of South Australia as far as Adelaide, have or had complex and elaborate systems of pronouns. People used different pronouns depending on: (1) the relationship between yourself and the person you were talking to, (2) the relationship between the two or more people you were talking about, and (3) the relationship between yourself and the people you were talking about. Bernhard Schebeck (1973) and Luise Hercus & Isobel White (1973) identified ten different series or kinds of pronouns in Adnyamathanha, that were each used with and about different kinds of kinfolk in different situations.

In his grammar of Barngarla, Schürmann identifies four pronoun series, and we'll look at each of these as we go along. However the system in Barngarla may have been more complex than this, and could have been closer to the system as it is seen in Adnyamathanha. There are gaps in Schürmann's description: for example while *budlanbi* 'they two' referred to a husband and wife, we don't know what pronoun referred to two people who were *not* husband and wife; or if perhaps *budlanbi* could have been used to refer to any two people.

3.1.3 1st Dual

The first set of dual pronouns appear to have been used generally; they may have been forms that you could use with people who weren't in any particular relationship to you:

First person dual – general

ngadli	ngadli	*we two, us two*
ngadluru	ngadlurhu	*ours, of us two*
ngadlidni	ngadlidni	*of or from us two*
ngadlidninge	ngadlidningi	*with us two*
ngadlidniru	ngadlidnirhu	*to us two*

Notice that there is no ergative shape here: non-singular pronouns in ergative, nominative and accusative functions all have the same shape in each person and number category. This situation is discussed below in Section 3.2.

The second set were used by a woman and her children: that is, by a woman and her son or daughter, a woman and her sister's son or daughter, or a man and his sister's son or daughter. For example if you were a woman and you wanted to refer to yourself and your son or daughter, you would use *ngadlaga* 'we two, us two.' If you were a man and you wanted to refer to yourself and your sister's son or daughter, you would also use *ngadlaga*. This is the set that Schebeck (1973: 13) and Hercus & White (1973: 58) call series-5 pronouns:

First person dual matrilineal – a woman and her child, a man and his sister's child

ngadlaga	ngadlaga	*we two, us two*
ngadlagguru	ngadlagurhu	*ours, of us two*
ngadlagadni	ngadlagadni	*of or from us two*
ngadlagadninge	ngadlagadningi	*with us two*
ngadlagadniru	ngadlagadnirhu	*to us two*

A third set were used by a man and his children: that is, a man and his son or daughter, a man and his brother's son or daughter, or a woman and her brother's son or daughter. If you were a man and you wanted to refer to yourself and your son or daughter, you would use *ngarinyi* 'we two, us two.' If you were a woman and you wanted to refer to yourself and your brother's son or daughter, you would also use *ngarinyi*:

First person dual patrilineal – a man and his child, a woman and her brother's child

ngarrinye	ngarinyi	*we two, us two*
ngarrinyuru	ngarinyurhu	*ours, of us two*
ngarrinyidni	ngarinyidni	*of or from us*
ngarrinyidninge	ngarinyidningi	*with us*
ngarrinyidniru	ngarinyidnirhu	*to us*

These shapes are clearly comparable with the patrilineal-pair forms found in Kuyani as *ngarinya* 'we two, father and child' (Hercus 2006a), and in Adnyamathanha as the series-9 pronoun *ngarinyi* (Schebeck 1973: 15-16, Hercus & White 1973: 59).

3.1.4 1st Plural

The 1st plural (we, us) shapes that Schürmann has left us seem to be based on the father-and-child series shown above. We don't know whether in Barngarla they were used only by fathers and their children, or if they were generalized for use by anyone:

First person plural

ngarrinyelbo	ngarinyarlbu	*we, us*
ngarrinyelburu	ngarinyarlburhu	*our, ours, of us*
ngarrinyelbudni	ngarinyarlbudni	*of or from us*
ngarrinyelbudningi	ngarinyarlbudningi	*with us*
ngarrinyelbudniru	ngarinyarlbudnirhu	*to us*

The alternative ablative, comitative and allative shapes based on the ablative ending *-urni* are as follow:

ngarrinyelburni	ngarinyarlburni	*of or from us*
ngarrinyelburninge	ngarinyarlburningi	*with us*
ngarrinyelburniru	ngarinyarlburnirhu	*to us*

Adnyamathanha has *ngarinyurlpa* 'father and children' (McEntee & McKenzie 1992: 40), clearly showing that the corresponding Barngarla word had a retroflex lateral.

3.1.5 2nd Singular

Second person singular – general

ninna	nhina	*you; NOMINATIVE*
nunno	nhurnu	*you; ERGATIVE*
nunko	nhunku	*your, yours*
nunkurni	nhunkurni	*of or from you*
nunkurninge	nhunkurningi	*with you*
nunkurniru	nhunkurnirhu	*towards you*

The shape of 2nd singular nominative pronoun was almost certainly *nhina*, as this form is widespread in the northern Thura-Yura languages.

In another series, a 2nd singular pronoun *nhurru* was used by a man when talking to his child, by a child when talking to his or her father, by a woman when talking to her brother's child, and by a child when talking to his or her father's sister. Notice that in this singular pronoun the ergative shape is the same as the nominative:

Second person singular patrilineal – a man to his child, a woman to her brother's child

nuro	nhurru	*you; NOMINATIVE*
nuro	nhurru	*you; ERGATIVE*[9]
nurko	nhurrgu	*your, yours*

---

[9] This layout follows Schürmann's on his page 11.

nurkurni	nhurrgurni	*of or from you*
nurkurninge	nhurrgurningi	*with you*
nurkurniru	nhurrgurnirhu	*towards you*

Schürmann records these pronouns as being used by 'a father and his children addressing each other.' Based on what we know about kinship systems in other northern Thura-Yura languages, it seems likely that these forms could used by women addressing their brothers' children as well.

Adnyamathanha and Kuyani have 2nd plural *nhura*, so we may assume for the time being that a stem shape *nhur-* or *nhurr-* is represented at this point in Schürmann's grammar. It is usual for plural forms to be used with singular reference in respect registers, as was the case in Wirangu at least (Hercus 1999: 79-80). The Western Desert variety Kukarta, spoken to the northwest of Barngarla, has *nyurra* for the 2nd singular pronoun (Platt 1972: 48).

The Western Desert variety I am spelling Kukarta is also spelled Kukata, Kokata, Gugada, and so on. Platt (1972: 3, 1967) points out that these terms may actually refer to two distinct Western Desert varieties, one with a label containing a dental stop, as /kukatha/, also written Gugadja or Kokatha, and another, the subject of his grammar, with a label containing an alveolar or retroflex stop: /kukarta/. As Platt notes on his page 3: 'there often seemed to be a tendency towards retroflexion, hence probably such spellings as Koogurda by Daisy Bates.' Being Irish, and so familiar with rhotic varieties of English, Bates frequently heard the rhoticization in retroflexed consonants with considerable accuracy.

3.1.6 Rhotic neutralization

Going by available material, Adnyamathanha and Kuyani allow the rhotic tap *r*, but not the trill *rr*, to appear in front of *k (g)*. Hercus (1999: 40) does not recognize a *r/rr+g* cluster in Wirangu, although it certainly occurs there, as *burgu/burku* 'dew, mist' demonstrates (Hercus 1999: 159). I suspect that the distinction between the trill and the tap may be neutralized in front of *k* in these languages. Nevertheless it is possible or indeed likely that a rhotic tap would have had a stop allophone in front of *g*, which might have made it hard for Schürmann to hear, as a rhotic. I will therefore represent the sound he heard in this environment by the trill symbol.

And for consistency, I will represent the shape of the root morpheme as also containing a trill, as *nhurru*.

3.1.7 2nd Singular forms

By comparison with the nominative form, the 2nd singular general ergative pronoun should be *nhunu*. Kuyani and Adnyamathanha have *nhuntu*, and Kaurna had *ninthu* (although *nhintu** might be equally plausible, by comparison with the northern form). No ergative shape is recorded for Nhukunu. Wirangu had an early shape *nhurni** (Hercus 1999: 77), but this was a nominative, not an ergative form. The choice of second nasal, then, boils down to a choice between the Barngarla *(nhina)* and Wirangu *(nhurni)* nominative shapes. Perhaps arbitrarily, I will presume that Barngarla might have patterned with Wirangu in this, and will assume for present purposes that the ergative 2nd singular pronoun may have been *nhurnu*.

The shape of the possessive 2nd singular pronoun is equally unclear. Adnyamathanha, Nhukunu and Kuyani all have *nhungku* (McEntee & McKenzie 1992: 53, Hercus 1992: 26, Hercus 2006a); Wirangu had a traditional (unreconstructed) shape *nhunyuku* (Hercus 1999: 78), and Kaurna had a shape that Teichelmann & Schürmann spelled *ninko*, and which Amery & Simpson (2013: 136) recast as *ninku*. Schürmann's representations of nasals before *k* appear to be consistent and reliable: he has *manka* 'tattoo scars (cicatrices)' where Kuyani has *minka* 'scar' (Hercus 2006c); and *manku-* 'take, receive' where Kuyani also has *manku* 'get, grab' (Hercus 2006a), and where Adnyamathanha has *marnku* 'grab, sieze (McEntee & McKenzie 1992: 77). Elsewhere his *ngk* sequences agree with those of other Thura-Yura languages: Barngarla *nhunggu-* 'give' compares with Kuyani *yungku-* and *nhungku-*, and with Adnyamathanha *nhungku-* (McEntee & McKenzie 1992: 53). Hercus & White (1973: 61) recorded the language name as *Banggarla* from Adnyamathanha speakers, which implies that Adnyamathanha *ngk* sequences could in some instances correspond to Barngarla *rng/nk* sequences. With this in mind I will trust Schürmann's transcription on this issue, and assume that the Barngarla 2nd singular possessive shape was *nhunku*, as he indicates. The same considerations will apply to the possessive shape of the interrogative pronoun *nganha* in Chapter Nine.

3.1.8 2nd Dual

Second person dual – general

nuwalla	nhuwala	*you two*
nuwalluru	nhuwalurhu	*your two, yours*
nuwallidni	nhuwalidni	*of or from you two*
nuwallidninge	nhuwalidningi	*with you two*
nuwallidniru	nhuwalidnirhu	*to you two*

Kuyani has a general-form 2nd singular pronoun *nhuwara*, and Adnyamathana has a form *nhuwalla* (sic), and others with stem shapes *nhuwat-* and *nhuwad-* (Hercus & White 1973: 58-59, Schebeck 1973: 12-14). I will on this basis assume that the lateral sound in the Barngarla word is apico-alveolar.

Second person dual matrilineal – a woman and her child, a man and his sister's child

nuwadnaga	nhuwadnaga	*you two*
nuwadnagguru	nhuwadnagurhu	*your two, yours*
nuwadnagadni	nhuwadnagadni	*of or from you two*
nuwadnagadninge	nhuwadnagadningi	*with you two*
nuwadnagadniru	nhuwadnagadnirhu	*to you two*

Both Adnyamathanha (Schebeck 1973: 13) and Kuyani have *nhuwadnaka* with this meaning. Kuyani even has *nhuwadnakarhunha* for the possessive shape.

Second person dual patrilineal – a man and his child, a woman and her brother's child

nuwarinye	nhuwarinyi	*you two*
nuwarinyuru	nhuwarinyurhu	*your two, yours*
nuwarinyidni	nhuwarinyidni	*of or from you two*
nuwarinyidninge	nhuwarinyidningi	*with you two*
nuwarinyidniru	nhuwarinyidnirhu	*to you two*

Shapes with the ending *-rinyi* also mark the *first* person dual pronouns with father-and-child meaning (see above), and Adnyamathanha has *nhuwadnanyi* for this 2nd dual meaning.

3.1.9 2nd Plural

Second person plural

nuralli	nhurali	*you all*
nuralluru	nhuralurhu	*your, yours*
nurallidni	nhuralidni	*of or from you all*
nurallidninge	nhuralidningi	*with you all*
nurallidniru	nhuralidnirhu	*to you all*

Adnyamathanha and Kuyani have 2nd plural *nhura,* and we may assume that the following lateral consonant is apico-alveolar, by analogy with that of the general 2nd dual pronoun *nhuwala* (see above).

3.1.10 3rd Singular

Third person singular

panna	banha	*he, him, she, her, it;* NOMINATIVE
padlo	badlu	*he, she;* ERGATIVE
parnüntyuru	barnundyurhu	*his, hers*
parnüntyudni	barnundyudni	*of, from him/her*
parnüntyudninge	barnundyudningi	*with him/her*
parnüntyudniru	barnundyudnirhu	*to him/her*

Kuyani has *panha* 'this,' Wirangu has *banha* 'he, she' (Hercus 1999: 83), and Kaurna had ergative *padlu* 'he, she' and possessive *parnu* 'his, hers' (Amery & Simpson 2013: 135). From these forms we can safely reconstruct the Barngarla shapes.

3.1.11 3rd Dual

Third person dual

pudlanbi	budlanbi	*they two, them two*
pudlanbiru	budlanbirhu	*their*
pudlanbidni	budlanbidni	*of or from them two*
pudlanbidninge	budlanbidningi	*with them two*
pudlanbidniru	budlanbidnirhu	*to them two*

This fourth set of dual pronouns referred to two people who were husband and wife: *budlanbi* 'they two, them two' is, as Schürmann says, 'more especially used for husband and wife.' The shapes shown here are unproblematic; the form *pula* is used for third person dual meaning widely in Australia, and Barngarla uses this shape with pre-stopping on the lateral.

Schürmann's vocabulary shows a 3rd dual pronoun *pannalbelli / banhalbili* 'they two,' which could most likely be used for any two people, regardless of kin relationships. This pronoun contains the dual suffix *-lbili* used also on nouns (see Section 7.2 below).

3.1.12 3rd Plural

Third person plural

yardna	yardna	*they, them*
yardnakkuru	yardnagurhu	*their, theirs*
yardnakudni	yardnagudni	*of or from them*
yardnakudninge	yardnagudningi	*with them*
yardnakudniru	yardnagudnirhu	*to them*

For this pronoun Kuyani has *thadna*, and Adnyamathanha has *yadna*. There is no apparent reason not to trust Schürmann's perception of retroflexion in the Barngarla form. This set of pronouns features a segment *-rdnagu* that is reminiscent of the segments *-dlaga* and *-dnaga* that we saw in the first and second person dual mother-and-child pronouns above. However there is no suggestion in Schürmann's text that these shapes are restricted to groups of mothers and their children, nor to uncles and their nephews.

3.2 Case marking

In these pronouns you will have noticed a pattern of endings, something like what follows, shown here with their technical labels:

–dhu , –nu , –ru , –dlu		ERGATIVE
no ending		NOMINATIVE
–rhu	*somebody's*	POSSESSIVE
–dni	*from somebody*	ABLATIVE
–dningi	*with somebody*	COMITATIVE
–dnirhu	*to somebody*	ALLATIVE

The ending *-dni* or *-rdni* by itself means 'from:' Schürmann says it 'differ[s] from [*-rhu*] by indicating the origin of a thing rather than the possession of it.' As an example he gives the sentence below:

(3.1)	paru	kattika	ngappardni
(g5)	barhu	gadiga	Ngabardni
	barhu	gadi-ga	Ngaba-rdni
	meat	bring-IMP	NAME-from

fetch meat of Ngapa

This was how this kind of sentence was expressed in English in the early nineteenth century: we would now say *get some meat* from *Ngapa*, without using the preposition *of*.

Kuyani has both *parlu* and *paaru* for 'meat/animal/game' (Hercus 2006a), Nhukunu has *partu* and *paru* (Hercus 1992: 26), Harry Crawford had *partu* (O'Grady 2001: 298), Wirangu has *baRu* (Miller et al 2010: 7) and Adnyamathanha has *vaarlu* (Tunstill 2004: 425). Three out of these six words have a retroflex sonorant *(rl, rh)*, two have the alveolar obstruent *r*, and two occurrences have the retroflex obstruent *rt*. Hercus (1999: 10-13) makes a case for a close link between Wirangu and Barngarla, especially in the south. For these reasons, then, I will tentatively suppose that the Barngarla word that Schürmann spells *paru* 'meat' had a retroflex rhotic as its second consonant, and will spell it here accordingly as *barhu*.

We can note that the possessive ending *-rhu* appears also in the allative ending *-dnirhu*: this is common in the Thura-Yura languages, and in Australia generally. We can also note that the segment *-dni* is part of the construction of the comitative and allative endings, as well as being on its own the ablative ending. We will look at this shape again in Sections 7.5.3 & 7.5.4.

With regard to the core cases, usually in Australia ergative, nominative and accusative, the Barngarla system of pronoun marking appears to be somewhat unusual. While being closest to Dixon's Stage A (as discussed in Dixon 2002: 299-315, 515-520), it shows significant differences. It is certainly different from the Adnyamathanha system, which is claimed to show ergative alignment exclusively in its nouns and pronouns (Dixon 2002: 519). Schürmann makes it clear that Barngarla non-singular pronouns display no core case-marking at all: he states that 'the nominative or first case of the above pronouns answers also for the dative and accusative cases,' and his verb paradigms and sentence examples bear this out.

Most *singular* pronouns, however, show ergative alignment; to recapitulate:

	nominative	ergative
1 sg	ngayi	ngadhu
2 sg	nhina	nhurnu
3 sg	banha	badlu

The exception to be seen in Schürmann's grammar is the 2nd singular patrilineal pronoun *nhurru*, which patterns like the non-singular pronouns in showing no core case-marking morphology. The upshot of this is that while intransitive and transitive verbs require distinct shapes for their singular subject pronouns (nominative and ergative respectively), there is no such requirement for non-singular pronouns:

the same shapes are used as subjects of both intransitive *and* transitive verbs, as well as as objects of transitive verbs.

A second pattern to be observed again involves the singular pronouns only. This pattern sees a distinction between the shapes of the core cases (ergative and nominative) on the one hand, and those of the oblique cases (all the rest) on the other. In these pronouns the oblique case stems are all based on the possessive shape, which is different from the core case stems. Also seen here are suggested forms for the dative case of singular pronouns, based on the nominative stem, and on the one attested example we have, *ngayini* 'to me:'

	nominative	ergative	possessive/oblique	dative
1 sg	ngayi	ngadhu	ngadyi	ngayini
2 sg	nhina	nhurnu	nhunku	(nhinani)
2 sg patrilineal	nhurru	nhurru	nhurrgu	(nhurruni)
3 sg	banha	badlu	barnu-ndyu-	(banhani)

In the 1st singular and in both 2nd singular forms the possessive shape serves as a stem for the further inflection of the oblique cases ablative, comitative and allative.

The 3rd singular shape is exceptional here, in that the possessive form is *barnundyurhu*: this word being composed of an historical root *barnu-* with a stem *-ndyu-* to which are then attached the possessive and ablative shapes.

The 3rd plural shape follows the 3rd singular pronoun in that the oblique stem is composed of the non-oblique root *yardna* followed by a stem element *-gu-*, to which are then attached the possessive and ablative endings:

	non-oblique	possessive/oblique
3 plural	yardna	yardna-gu-

As mentioned above, a third pattern to be observed is that while for singular pronouns the ablative, comitative and allative cases use the possessive shape as a stem, for all pronouns the comitative and allative cases in turn use the ablative shape as a stem. This pattern can be summarized as follows:

	SINGULAR		NON-SINGULAR
STEM 1	STEM 2		STEM 3
possessive shape	possessive+ablative shape		ablative shape
eg: *ngadyi*	*ngadyi-dni*		*ngadli-dni*
↓	↓		↓
ablative attachment	comitative, allative attachment		comitative, allative attachment

The stem-2 and stem-3 shapes are able to host other suffixes as well, such as ASSOCIATIVE *-lyga: ngadyidnilyga* 'with me, on my account.' The 3rd singular and 3rd plural pronouns display a variation on the singular pattern, as noted.

Four: Intransitive verbs

4.1 Introduction

Barngarla verbs are composed of a base or ROOT, to which are added various endings or suffixes that show when and sometimes how the event or act portrayed by the verb is being performed. Barngarla verb roots that are not derived from other words (such as nouns or adjectives) usually, or at least very often, contain two syllables. Verbs will be cited either as Schürmann cites them, in a non-past (present and future) tense shape such as *ngugadha* 'go,' or as a root, like *nguga-* 'go.'

4.1.1 Verb roots

A few apparently underived verbs discussed in this commentary show trisyllabic roots, such as: *babmandi-* 'come,' *yurrulbu-* 'accompany,' *gurrugu-* 'be giddy,' *barlaga-ri-* 'rise, hasten' (listed in Schürmann's vocabulary with the derivational suffix *-ri-* (see Section 10.2.2 below)), *wandhaga-* 'leave behind,' and *iridni-* 'separate.' There may, however, be explanations for some of these. The segment *ndi* on the end of *babmandi-* looks like a Thura-Yura present-tense ending frozen onto the root of this verb. The segments *bu* and *ga* on the ends of *yurrulbu-, wandhaga-* and *barlaga-* look like Pama-Nyungan verb formatives likewise frozen onto these root shapes. They may be relics from a time when as verb formatives those shapes were productive in Barngarla, or they may be borrowed more recently. The fact that the Kuyani equivalent of Barngarla *wandhaga-* is *wantha-,* would tend to support the supposition that these are augmentations of what were originally disyllabic roots. The root *gurrugu-* is probably ideophonic. In the dictionary four underived, trisyllabic roots end in the segment *mbi-*, two in *bma-*, and one in *mba-*, as if these shapes too could be, or could have been, formatives of some sort.

A full review of Schürmann's vocabulary would doubtless reveal more multisyllabic roots, and may suggest other explanations for their occurrence. For example, the four-syllable root *garradyugu-* 'hold up to the wind, winnow' is composed of the adjective *garra* 'high' prefixed to a bisyllablic root *dyugu-*. And it is possible that the stem *barlaga-ri-* 'rise, hasten' referred to above may actually be constructed of a disyllabic root *barla-* and a (possibly archaic) iterative stem *-gari-* (cf Section 4.4.4), perhaps frozen onto the root to make a stem *barla-gari-*. Southern varieties of the Western Desert Language such as Tjuparn use *-karri-* as an iterative stem (Clendon 2011). Further examination of Schürmann's vocabulary will be needed to confirm or discredit this suggestion.

4.1.2 Transitivity

The difference between transitive and intransitive verbs is essential and basic to Barngarla grammar, and is a point of grammar you will need to know about. Most English verbs can be given or forced into transitive expressions, although there are a few that are always, or nearly always, intransitive, such as *chatter, giggle, die, sleep,* and *snore*. A transitive verb is one that has an object, as has the verb *saw* in *I saw the light,* where *I* is the subject and *the light* is the object. An intransitive verb is one that has *no* object, such as the verb *chatter* in *they won't stop chattering,* where *they* is the subject, and there is no object. In Barngarla you need to make *nominative-*case nouns and singular pronouns (such as *ngayi* 'I') the subjects of *intransitive* verbs. And you need to make *ergative-*case nouns and singular pronouns (such as *ngadhu* 'I') the subjects of *transitive* verbs. The terms *nominative* and *ergative* are discussed in Section 3.1.1. Schürmann refers to transitive verbs as *active* verbs, and to intransitive verbs as *neuter* verbs; these are the terms you will see in his vocabulary.

4.2 Present-tense verbs

4.2.1 The present suffix

In this section we'll look at the Barngarla intransitive verb *nguga-* 'go.' The first set of shapes we'll look at are those that mark present and future tense. This tense in Barngarla is like the so-called present tense in English, where *I'm going to the shop* can refer to present time (I am now in the act of walking to the shop) or to future time (I will be going to the shop sometime soon).

Schürmann writes the present-tense ending as *-ta, -tta, -tu* and *-ti*. We will have to look at both the consonant *t/tt* and the vowels *a, i* and *u* in order to make sense of these endings.

Harry Crawford gave present-tense verbs ending in *-tha* (see Chapter Six), so we may assume that this is the shape of the ending that Schürmann recorded. Crawford's Iron Knob forms, moreover, can be checked against other records of Thura-Yura languages.

Luise Hercus (1999: 95) provides a summary of Thura-Yura present tense endings. Where we can discern them, and using Amery & Simpson's (2013: 123) grammar of Kaurna, the stop consonants involved in this meaning can be sorted out as follows:

lamino-palatal *(-ty-/-dy-)*	Nharangga	-dja
	Nhukunu	-tya
	Kuyani	-tya, -ntya
lamino-dental *(-th-/-dh-)*	Kaurna	-nthi
	Wirangu	-dha
	Adnyamathanha	-tha, -ntha
apico-alveolar *(-t-/-d-)*	Adnyamathanha	-ta, -nta
	Kuyani	-ta, -nta

We have no contemporary information about this shape in Nhawu or Ngadyuri. The Wirangu present tense ending is *-rn/-n,* but the POTENTIAL mood uses *-dha*, a shape which corresponds, as Hercus (1999: 111) points out, to the present tense shapes in other Thura-Yura languages.

From this list it appears that a laminal or dental consonant *(-dy-* or *-dh-)* was most common across the Thura-Yura area. In the far north of the area, north of the Flinders Ranges, Kuyani used both *-ty-* and *-t-*. To the south of Kuyani, Adnyamathanha too appears to be on the borderline where the *-th-/-ty-* forms and the *-t-* forms meet, as Adnyamathanha also uses both shapes.

From this comparison across the Thura-Yura area we can be certain that the Barngarla present tense ending used *-dh-*, and in this way patterned like most of the other Thura-Yura languages, particularly those south of the Flinders Ranges. This opinion is more credible when we remember that the variety of Barngarla that Schürmann recorded was spoken far to the south, around Port Lincoln at the southern end of the Eyre Peninsula.

4.2.2 Kuyani & Adnyamathanha forms

Hercus (2006c) states that the two endings recorded in Kuyani do not appear to differ in meaning. Neither is it clear to me whether the use of both *-t-* and *-th-* in the Adnyamathanha present-tense ending is (1) lexical, that is, different verbs select different endings, (2) dialectal, that is, different families use different endings, (3) allomorphic, that is, the shape of the verb stem, or some semantic property of the verb root, conditions which ending is used, or (4) in free variation: this appears to be the explanation offered by Andrew Coulthard (Schebeck 1974: 25), and agrees with Hercus' observation for Kuyani.

4.2.3 Vowel harmony

Barngarla is unusual for a Thura-Yura language in at least two ways: the first is in showing a phenomenon called *vowel harmony:* this is when the vowels in one part of a word rhyme or harmonize with the vowels in another part next to it. The Barngarla present tense ending seems always to have harmonized or rhymed with the final vowel of its verb stem. That is, the ending was *-dha, -dhi* or *-dhu,* depending on the verb it was attached to:

SCHÜRMANN	PHONEMIC	ENGLISH
wanggata	wangg**a**dh**a**	*speak, talk*
nungkutu	nhungg**u**dh**u**	*give*
worniti	warn**i**dh**i**	*fall*

Notice how the vowel at the end of the word is the same as the vowel at the end of the verb stem.

4.2.4 Subject agreement

To say *I go/I will go/I'm going*, then, you may put the nominative case pronoun *ngayi* 'I' in front of the present tense shape of the verb *nguga-* 'go,' to make: *ngayi ngugadha* 'I'm going.' The following list shows how all three persons and all three numbers are formed, for Barngarla present-tense verbs:

		SCHÜRMANN	PHONEMIC	ENGLISH
Sg:	1	ngai ngukata	ngayi ngugadha	*I'm going, I'll go, I go*
	2	ninna ngukata	nhina ngugadha	*you go*
	3	panna ngukatawo	banha ngugadhawu	*he or she goes*
Du:	1	ngadli ngukata	ngadli ngugadha	*we two go*
	2	nuwalla ngukamatta	nhuwala ngugamadha	*you two go*
	3	pudlanbi ngukamatta	budlanbi ngugamadha	*they two go*
Pl:	1	ngarrinyelbo ngukata	ngarinyarlbu ngugadha	*we go*
	2	nuralli ngukatanna	nhurali ngugadhanha	*you all go*
	3	yardna ngukatanna	yardna ngugadhanha	*they go*

Barngarla is also unusual for a Thura-Yura language in that the shape of a verb changes in accordance with its subject:

(1) The 3rd singular subject shape ends in *-wu;* this is extrapolated from Schürmann's *-wo* (see discussion in Section 2.3). Adnyamathanha has a 3rd singular nominative ending *-wa* on verbs (Schebeck 1974: 30), comparable to Barngarla *-wu*. In his grammar Schürmann has the verb:

(4.1) padnatawudlu

(g22) badnadhawudlu

badna-dha-wu-dlu

go-PRES-3.sg.NOM-DOUBT

he/she/it may go/be

which clearly shows the 3rd singular nominative shape as *-wu* spelled phonemically when it is not at the end of a word.

(2) The 2nd dual- and 3rd dual subject verbs have a segment *-ma-* IN FRONT OF the tense ending, making a dual ending *-ma-dha;* note that this ending is not available for 1st dual forms.

(3) Schürmann's 2nd plural- and 3rd plural subject forms end in *-nna*. We have no analogue for this ending in other languages, but the suffix *-nha* is found in a wide variety of uses in Thura-Yura languages, and it is possible that this shape was used here as well. Note however that Kaurna has a plural ending *-rna,* although this is attached to nouns, not verbs (Amery & Simpson 2013: 123). This shape could conceivably be a truncation of 3rd plural *yardna,* as non-prestopped *-rna,* but Harry Crawford's *pirdnanha (?pirdananha)* (see Chapter Six) would seem to support the interpretation offered here. Schürmann is usually accurate in recognizing and representing the apical (alveolar/post-alveolar) contrast. The ending here transcribed *-nha* occurs AFTER the tense ending.

(4) We will find that the shapes *-ma-* and *-nha* regularly mark dual and plural subjects respectively, for second and third persons on Barngarla verbs that do NOT have pronoun suffixes attached.

4.3 Pronoun suffixes

Schürmann points out that verbal expressions like those seen above in Section 4.2.4 may be formed in the same way as they are in other Thura-Yura languages: that is, by putting some form of the subject pronoun *after* the verb, and attaching it *to* the verb. He states: 'the natives very commonly pronounce the pronoun after the verb and more or less contract the two into one word.' Here is an example he gives:

    ngukatai → ngugadhayi   *I go or shall go (g22)*

This is a contraction of *ngugadha ngayi*.

Hercus & White (1973: 60) and Schebeck (1974: 30) have discussed this phenomenon in Adnyamathanha, although they are not clear about how much of the pronoun gets knocked off when this happens. Schebeck claims the initial consonant or the first syllable may be dropped, while Hercus & White say that 'these bound forms [pronouns] are generally identical with the free forms except for the loss of the initial consonant.' As an example using the verb *nguka-* 'go,' they offer:

    ADNYAMATHANHA: ngukardupa *they two are going*

This is a contraction of *nguka* 'go' and *valardupa* 'they two:' but we can see that it is not just the first consonant of the pronoun that is lost, but the first two syllables. And we don't know whether the sound *a* in the middle of *ngukardupa* is the *a* at the end of *nguka,* or an *a* from *valardupa*. There is therefore quite a lot of uncertainty as to exactly how pronouns are joined to the ends of verbs, in Thura-Yura languages.

Nevertheless and thanks to Schürmann's clarity and carefulness, it is possible to make a reasonable assessment of how this system worked in Barngarla:

		SCHÜRMANN	SHORT FORM	ENGLISH
Sg:	1	ngukatai *or* ngukatia	ngugadhayi, ngugadhiya	*I'm going*
	2	ngukatinni	ngugadhini	*you go*
	3	ngukatao	ngugadhawu	*he or she goes*
Du:	1	ngukatadli	ngugadhadli	*we two go*
	2	ngukatuwalla	ngugadhuwala	*you two go*
	3		(ngugamadha)	*they two go*
Pl:	1	ngukatarrinyelbo	ngugadharinyarlbu	*we go*
	2	ngukaturalli	ngugadhurali	*you all go*
	3	ngukatardna	ngugadhardna	*they go*

Note that in these forms the second and third person dual and plural markers *-ma-* and *-nha* do not occur.

Writing about the short forms presented here, Schürmann explains that 'the other tenses [are] to be formed in a similar manner.' And from now on we will have to take him at his word, because he records only a few examples of short-form verbs.

Although Schürmann leaves the 3rd dual short-form line blank in his grammar, it is reasonable to suppose that the long-form *-madha* ending could be used with this interpretation *(ngugamadha)*, just as the long-from shape with the 3rd singular *-wu* ending *(ngugadhawu)* is used for the 3rd singular short form.

Note as well that because of Schürmann's careful recording, we can answer at least one of the questions we asked above. In Barngarla at least, it is the last vowel of the verb, as well as the first consonant of the pronoun, that are lost when a subject pronoun is suffixed to a verb to make a short form:

<u>ngugadh</u>a n<u>hina</u> → ngugadhini *you go*

<u>ngugadh</u>a n<u>huwala</u> → ngugadhuwala *you two go*

The singular shape *ngugadhini* has its final vowel *a* harmonized to *i*.

It would seem that *any* of the subject (nominative and ergative) pronouns we have looked at in Chapter Three can be attached to a verb on its right-hand side to show the verb's subject, not just the ones that Schürmann offers in his lists. For example, Schürmann provides the following sentence, using the 1st dual mother-and-child (matrilineal) pronoun *ngadlaga*, shortened to *-adlaga*, rather than the general 1st dual pronoun *ngadli* (shortened to *-adli*) shown above:

(4.2) pappidnuru   ngukat' adlaga,   ngammiá

(g12) babidnurhu   ngugadhadlaga,   ngamiya

       babi-dnurhu   nguga-dha-adlaga   ngami-ya

       father-toward   go-PRES-1.du.MATR.NOM   mother-VOC

to father let us two go, mother

This sentence shows the vocative ending *-ya* on *ngami* 'mother.' This is an ending you may attach when talking to someone, or calling out to someone; it is found as well in Adnyamathanha (Schebeck 1974: 8).

Not only that, it is likely that pronouns in *any* grammatical function (subject, object, possessive, etc) could be suffixed to verbs. Here is a sentence example with a verb that appears to have a suffixed 1st dual pronoun *object;* no gloss is given, so I have had to provide one:

(4.3)   karpanga   iridningutu adli

(8)   garrbanga   iridningudhuwadli

        garrba-nga   iridni-ngu-dhu-w-adli

        house-ERG   separate-APPL-PRES-EP-1.du.NOM

the house/room separates us/keeps us apart

Kuyani has *iri-* 'move, shift, get out of the way, spread out' (Hercus 2006a), and Barngarla has *iridhi* 'move, be moving, shift,' which, as a verb of motion, is likely to correspond in part to Barngarla's intransitive *iridni-* 'separate.' For the derivation of the transitive verb *iridni-ngu-* 'separate,' see Section 10.7.

The following example shows a possessive-case singular pronoun marking a first-person recipient object:

(4.4)   mai   ngaitye   pulyo   kulakaitye

(g7)   mayi   ngadyi   pulyu   gulagadyi

        mayi   ngadyi   pulyu   gula-ga-adyi

        food   1.sg.POSS   little   cut-IMP-1.sg.POSS

cut me a little bread pray

Schürmann has *pulyo* 'small' and *kulata (guladha)* 'sever, cut, break, tear.' In this sentence the ending *-(a)dyi* on the verb is a short form of *ngadyi* 'to/for/of me.' In Adnyamathanha both free and bound forms of a pronoun may be found in the same sentence (Schebeck 1974: 31), and this is surely what we see here.

The phenomenon of non-subject pronouns suffixed to verbs is vanishingly rare in Schürmann's Barngarla vocabulary, but this is likely to be a result of the kinds of sentences he was exposed to, or which he selected to document, rather than being a feature of the language itself. Kaurna is able to have more than one pronoun suffix attached to a verb; that is, both subject and object pronouns are able to be stacked on the end of a verb together. The following Kaurna example is from Teichelmann & Schürmann (1840: 24, grammar section): [10]

KAURNA	tidnarla	nguiyuatturla
	tidnarla	nguyuathurla
	tidna-rla	nguyu-athu-rla
	foot-3.du	warm-1.sg.ERG-3.du.NOM

the feet, I will warm them

Here we see short forms of the Kaurna 1st singular ergative pronoun *ngathu* and the 3rd dual nominative pronoun *purla* occurring in sequence after a present optative shape of the verb *nguyu-* 'warm.' It is likely that this kind of arrangement was possible in Barngarla too, although it may not have been all that common.

4.4 Other tenses, aspects & moods

4.4.1 Past tense

The following shapes of the verb *nguga-* 'go' are used to signal past tense. Schürmann called these shapes 'imperfect or preterite,' which means that these verb forms signal past time without reference to whether the past event was completed or was on-going.

Because Schürmann recorded only a few short-form verbs for *nguga-*, I will have to reconstruct, hopefully plausibly, the shapes of the short forms for some of the other verbal meanings he offers:

---

[10] I am grateful to Clara Stockigt for bringing this Kaurna example to my attention, and to Rob Amery for help with glossing.

		SCHÜRMANN	PHONEMIC	ENGLISH
Sg:	1	ngai ngukanna	ngayi ngugana	*I went*
	2	ninna ngukanna	nhina ngugana	*you went*
	3	panna ngukannawo	banha nguganawu	*he or she went*
Du:	1	ngadli ngukanna	ngadli ngugana	*we two went*
	2	nuwalla ngukamanna	nhuwala ngugamana	*you two went*
	3	pudlanbi ngukamanna	budlanbi ngugamana	*they two went*
Pl:	1	ngarrinyelbo ngukanna	ngarinyarlbu ngugana	*we went*
	2	nuralli ngukanna	nhurali ngugana	*you all went*
	3	yardna ngukananna	yardna ngugananha	*they went*

		SHORT FORM	ENGLISH
Sg:	1	nguganayi, nguganiya	*I went*
	2	nguganini	*you went*
	3	nguganawu	*he or she went*
Du:	1	nguganadli	*we two went*
	2	nguganuwala	*you two went*
	3	(ngugamana)	*they two went*
Pl:	1	nguganarinyarlbu	*we went*
	2	nguganurali	*you all went*
	3	nguganardna	*they went*

Wirangu has a past tense suffix *-na* (Hercus 1999: 115), Kuyani has a tense suffix *-na* which is used for both present and past (Hercus 2006c), and Adnyamathanha and Kuyani have a past tense suffix *-nanta* (Schebeck 1974: 25, Hercus 1999: 111). On this basis we may reconstruct a past tense ending *-na* for Barngarla. Notice that it is likely that the 2nd-3rd plural ending *-nha* is placed after the tense-marker in the 3rd plural shape *ngugananha* 'they went.'

4.4.2 Imperative

Imperative verbs are the forms you use when you are telling someone to do something. The imperative verb ending in all Thura-Yura languages is *-ka* (cf eg Adnyamathanha, Schebeck 1974: 26), and this is what we find when you're telling one person to do something. When you're telling two people to do something, the ending you use is *-maga*, and when you're telling more than two people to do something you use the ending *-ganha*:

Sg:.	ngukakka	ngugaga	*go! you can go*
Du:	ngukamakka	ngugamaga	*you two go! you can both go*
pl.	ngukakanna	ngugaganha	*you all go! you can all go*

4.4.3 Hortative

A set of verbs with a somewhat similar meaning to imperative, seek to allow or enable someone to do something. These forms probably mean something like, *let (someone) do (something); (someone) can or may do (something)*:

Sg:	1	ngukai	ngugayi	*let me go, I can go*
	3	ngukawo	ngugawu	*let him go, he can go*
Du:	1	ngukamadli	ngugamadli	*let's both go, we can both go*
	3	ngukamai	ngugamayi	*let them both go*
Pl:	1	ngukarrinyelbo	ngugarinyarlbu	*let's go, we can go*
	3	nguka anna *or* ngukarna	nguga(y)anha *or* ngugarna	*let them go, they can go*

Notice that in this list there are no second person (you) forms. Although Schürmann included them in his list, they are in effect imperative forms, and I have put them up into the imperative list above.

These forms are called *hortative;* they allow or encourage or even require someone to do something. The hortative shapes in Barngarla appear to have short-form pronouns suffixed to a bare root, with the sound *y* evident in the 3rd dual and 3rd plural shapes. When we come to transitive verbs, we will see more evidence for the sound *y* occurring in third person forms. Here are two examples of how hortative verbs are used; note again how the 3rd singular nominative short-form pronoun -*wu* is attached directly onto the root of the verb *yuwa-* 'stand:'

(4.5a)   pityerki   yala   yuwao
(77)   bidyirrgi   yala   yuwawu

bidyirrgi   yala   yuwa-wu
wood   open   stand-3.sg.NOM

let the door stand open

(4.5b)   yarru   ikkai
(44)   yarru   igayi

yarru   iga-ayi
just   sit-1.sg.NOM

let me just sit down

The noun *bidyirrgi* denoted any smooth piece of wood, and may be related to Wirangu *bidyi* 'tree bark, bark dish;' Wirangu also has *yala* 'hole, hollow' (Miller et al 2010: 7, 90).

4.4.4 Iterative forms

Schürmann included two other 2nd singular forms in this list: they are as follows, with suggested interpretations:

Sg: 2	ngukannaka	nguganaga	*keep on going along! /*
	ngukakkaitye	ngugagadyi	*you can keep on going along*

These verbs include two suffixes, -*naga* and -*gadyi,* that may have been used with iterative meaning, as *go along while doing something; do something while going along.* In Adnyamathanha Tunbridge (1988: 272) describes the iterative suffix -*nangga* with this meaning, and in Wirangu Hercus (1999: 129) describes the iterative suffix -*gadi,* the same as the Western Desert shape -*kati,* again with the same meaning. It is just possible that Barngarla -*naga* may correspond to Adnyamathanha -*nangga,* and Barngarla -*gadyi* to Wirangu -*gadi.*

4.4.5 Desiderative

Another set of forms Schürmann calls 'intensive future.' Of this set he says, 'I have called this tense the intensive future for want of a more suitable name. The meaning of it is that the person ... is willing or resolved to do something.' These forms show a suffix -*ng*, and seem to mean that the subject wants to do something. Schürmann offers mostly short forms only:

Sg:	1	ngukangai	ngugangayi	*I want to go*
	2	ngukanginni	ngugangini	*you want to go*
	3	ngukanggawo	nguganggawu	*s/he wants to go*
Du:	1	ngukangadli	ngugangadli	*we two want to go*
	2	nuwalla ngukamangka	nhuwala ngugamangga	*you two want to go*
	3	pudlanbi ngukamangka	budlanbi ngugamangga	*they two want to go*
pl	1	ngukangarinyelbo	ngugangarinyarlbu	*we want to go*
	2	ngukangkanuralli	ngugangganhurali	*you all want to go*
	3	ngukangkardna	nguganggardna	*they want to go*

Rather than 'intensive future,' I will refer to these forms as *desiderative*, a term more commonly used to signal a verb form with volitional meaning.

4.4.6 Perfect aspect

Barngarla verbs with the ending -*ndya* signal a verbal aspect that is called 'perfect.' This meaning describes a state of being: while that state may have come into being in the past, it is still relevant to, important for, or ongoing into the present. For example: the sentence *John broke his arm* has simply a past-tense meaning; it describes an event that happened in the past. The perfect-aspect sentence *John has broken his arm* describes not so much an event, as a state of affairs that came into being sometime in the recent or not-so-recent past, and a state that continues into the present: if John has broken his arm, then we'd better do something about it. Schürmann's vocabulary gives examples of this kind of usage:

(4.6a) gadla   padluntyao
(50)   gardla   badlundyawu
        gardla   badlu-ndya-wu
        fire   die-PERF-3.sg.NOM

the fire is gone out

(4.6b) padluntyao   wibmangkalli?
(g7)   badlundyawu   wibmanggarli?
        badlu-ndya-wu   wibma-nggarli
        die-PERF-3.sg.NOM already-INTER

has he died already?

Kuyani has *padlu-* 'die' (Hercus 2006a), and Schürmann has *wibma* 'already;' although Kuyani has *wibma* 'song' (Hercus 2006a), and Adnyamathanha has *wibma* 'history' (McEntee & McKenzie 1992: 122). Kuyani has an historic past-tense marker *-ntyu* (Hercus 2006c), only formally related to the Barngarla shape.

This kind of sentence describes a present state of affairs that has come into being. The sentence in (4.6a) would normally be used when it is clear that a particular state of affairs (in this case the fire being out), is still important into the present (now we might get cold, now we can't see, now we've got nothing to cook on, etc).

The perfect-aspect verb-forms that Schürmann lists are as follows:

		SCHÜRMANN	PHONEMIC	ENGLISH
Sg:	1	ngai ngukaintya	ngayi ngugandya	*I have gone*
	2	ninna ngukaintya	nhina ngugandya	*you have gone*
	3	panna ngukaintyawo	banha ngugandyawu	*he or she has gone*
Du:	1	ngadli ngukaintya	ngadli ngugandya	*we have both gone*
	2	nuwalla ngukamantya	nhuwala ngugamandya	*you have both gone*
	3	pudlanbi ngukamantya	budlanbi ngugamandya	*they have both gone*

Pl:	1	ngarrinyelbo ngukaintya	ngarinyarlbu ngugandya		*we have gone*
	2	nuralli ngukaintyanna	nhurali ngugandyanha		*you have all gone*
	3	yardna ngukaintyanna	yardna ngugandyanha		*they have gone*

		SHORT FORM	ENGLISH
Sg:	1	ngugandyayi, ngugandyiya	*I have gone*
	2	ngugandyini	*you have gone*
	3	ngugandyawu	*he or she has gone*
Du:	1	ngugandyadli	*we have both gone*
	2	ngugandyuwala	*you have both gone*
	3	(ngugamandya)	*they have both gone*
Pl:	1	ngugandyarinyarlbu	*we have gone*
	2	ngugandyurali	*you have all gone*
	3	ngugandyardna	*they have gone*

4.4.7 Subjunctive present

Another form of intransitive verb Schürmann records, he calls 'subjunctive,' with a meaning *I might go, I would go, I could go, I should go*:

		SCHÜRMANN	PHONEMIC	ENGLISH
Sg:	1	ngai ngukara	ngayi ngugarha	*I might go*
	2	ninna ngukara	nhina ngugarha	*you might go*
	3	panna ngukarawo	banha ngugarhawu	*he or she might go*
Du:	1	ngadli ngukara	ngadli ngugarha	*we two might go*
	2	nuwalla ngukamara	nhuwala ngugamarha	*you two might go*
	3	pudlanbi ngukamara	budlanbi ngugamarha	*they two might go*
Pl:	1	ngarrinyelbo ngukara	ngarinyarlbu ngugarha	*we might go*

2	nuralli ngukaranna		nhurali ngugarhanha		*you all might go*
	or ngukarna		*or* ngugarna		
3	yardna ngukarna		yardna ngugarna		*they might go*

		SHORT FORM	ENGLISH
Sg:	1	ngugarhayi, ngugarhiya	*I might go*
	2	ngugarhini	*you might go*
	3	ngugarhawu	*he or she might go*
Du:	1	ngugarhadli	*we two might go*
	2	ngugarhuwala	*you two might go*
	3	(ngugamarha)	*they two might go*
Pl:	1	ngugarharinyarlbu	*we might go*
	2	ngugarhurali	*you all might go*
	3	ngugarhardna	*they might go*

Adnyamathanha has an irrealis ending *-rha* which Tunstill (2004: 429) describes as 'something that did not happen, or could have happened or will never happen,' and which Schebeck (1974: 26) presents with a sentence example he translates as *you should have hit him*. Hercus (2006a) notes the same ending in Kuyani, which she describes as 'may be, potential verbal affix,' with a sentence example translated as *they might come back,* which is entirely congruent with the meaning Schürmann provides for the verb form under consideration here. However Kuyani has another suffix *-ra* (Hercus 2006c), described as an irrealis marker, with a sentence example translated as *you should [quickly] go*. Both these suffixes mark irrealis meaning, and it is not clear to me that they are in fact different. However, it seems that the Kuyani ending *-Ra* most closely matches the meaning of the Barngarla verbs, and so I will propose that this is the form that Schürmann intended.

4.4.8 Subjunctive past

Finally, Schürmann lists past-tense subjunctive forms of the verb *nguga-*, with a meaning, *(someone) would have, might have, could have,* or *should have, done (something)*.

These verb forms use the perfect-aspect suffix *-ndya* followed by the subjunctive suffix *-rha* to make an ending *-ndyarha*. First we will look at the long forms: these may be seen in Table 4.1 at the end of this chapter. And now here are how the short forms may have been uttered:

		SHORT FORM	ENGLISH
Sg:	1	ngugandyarhayi, ngugandyarhiya	*I would have gone*
	2	ngugandyarhini	*you would have gone*
	3	ngugandyarhawu	*he or she would have gone*
Du:	1	ngugandyarhadli	*we would have both gone*
	2	ngugandyarhuwala	*you would have both gone*
	3	(ngugamandyarha)	*they would have both gone*
Pl:	1	ngugandyarharinyarlbu	*we would have gone*
	2	ngugandyarhurali	*you would have all gone*
	3	ngugandyarhardna	*they would have gone*

		SCHÜRMANN	PHONEMIC	MEANING
Sg:	1	ngai ngukaintyara	ngayi ngugandyarha	*I would have gone*
	2	ninna ngukaintyara	nhina ngugandyarha	*you would have gone*
	3	panna ngukaintyarawo	banha ngugandyarhawu	*he or she would have gone*
Dual:	1	ngadli ngukaintyara	ngadli ngugandyarha	*we would have both gone*
	2	nuwalla ngukamantyara	nhuwala ngugamandyarha	*you would have both gone*
	3	pudlanbi ngukamantyara	budlanbi ngugamandyarha	*they would have both gone*
Pl:	1	ngarrinyelbo ngukaintyara	ngarinyarlbu ngugandyarha	*we would have gone*
	2	nuralli ngukaintyaranna *or* ngukaintyarna	nhurali ngugandyarhanha *or* ngugandyarna	*you would have all gone*
	3	yardna ngukaintyaranna *or* ngukaintyarna	yardna ngugandyarhanha *or* ngugandyarna	*they would have gone*

Table 4.1: Subjunctive past forms of *nguka-* 'go'

Five: Transitive verbs

Transitive verbs are those that need an object; typically verbs such as *hitting*: you need to hit *something*; and you have to see *something*; to hear *something*; to catch *something*, and so on. Despite that, in English lots of verbs can be both intransitive *and* transitive: for example you can *eat chips* (with an object), or you can just *be eating* (with no stated object).

With transitive verbs in Barngarla, you need to use the ergative shapes of nouns, or the singular ergative pronouns *ngadhu* 'I,' *nhurnu* 'you' or *badlu* 'he, she' with, or in front of the verb.

Schürmann uses a verb that I will transcribe as *widi-* 'spear, pierce' to illustrate how transitive verbs work in Barngarla. Kuyani has *wityi-* 'to spear' (Hercus 2006a), and Wirangu has *widyirn* 'throw a weapon' (Miller et al 2010: 86). Adnyamathanha has *witi-* 'to spear' (McEntee & McKenzie 1992: 120), and also *withi-* 'spear, stake' (that is, impale with a stick into the ground) (McEntee & McKenzie 1992: 121). I will assume that the first Adnyamathanha verb corresponds most closely to the one that Schürmann uses to exemplify the conjugation of transitive verbs.

5.1 Present tense

Here are the long forms of the present/future tense of the verb *widi-*, showing the ending *-dhi* harmonizing with the last vowel in the verb root. Note that while the singular pronouns are marked for ergative case, the non-singular pronouns are the same as those used with the intransitive verb *nguga-*; that is, they do not display case-marking here:

		SCHÜRMANN	PHONEMIC	ENGLISH
Sg:	1	ngatto wittiti	ngadhu wididhi	*I'm spearing*
	2	nunno wittiti	nhurnu wididhi	*you spear*
	3	padlo wittitarru	badlu wididharu	*he or she spears*
Du:	1	ngadli wittiti	ngadli wididhi	*we two spear*
	2	nuwalla wittimatta	nhuwala widimadha	*you two spear*
	3	padlanbi wittimatta	budlanbi widimadha	*they two spear*
Pl:	1	ngarrinyelbo wittiti	ngarinyarlbu wididhi	*we spear*
	2	nuralli wittitanna	nhurali wididhanha	*you all spear*
	3	yardna wittitanna	yardna wididhanha	*they spear*

Again, there are a few things we can note about these forms:

(1) Note again the segment *-ma-* in the 2nd dual and 3rd dual subject shapes, and the ending *-nha* in the 2nd plural and 3rd plural subject shapes, again only in verbs that do NOT have pronoun suffixes attached.

(2) The present-tense suffix, which is *-dhi* on most forms, goes to *-dha* when it comes in front of *-(a)ru* and *-(a)nha*, and also when it comes after *-ma-*,

(3) Instead of the intransitive 3rd singular subject ending *-wo (-wu)*, Schürmann has a transitive 3rd singular subject ending he spells *-rru*. The phonemic form of this ending needs some discussion (see Section 5.2 below),

(4) Note that for the 3rd dual pronoun Schürmann here has *padlanbi:* this is surely a typo, as this word is *pudlanbi* in every other transitive list.

Schürmann also gives us the short-form versions of this transitive verb, as shown below. And again, note how the second- and third-person dual and plural subject-marking shapes *-ma-* and *-nha* are absent from these short-form verbs:

		SCHÜRMANN	SHORT FORM	ENGLISH
Sg:	1	wittitatto	wididhadhu	*I'm spearing*
	2	wittitunno	wididhurnu	*you spear*
	3	wittitarru	wididharu	*he or she spears*
Du:	1	wittitadli	wididhadli	*we two spear*
	2	wittituwalla	wididhuwala	*you two spear*
	3		(widimadha)	*they two spear*
Pl:	1	wittitarrinyelbo	wididharinyarlbu	*we spear*
	2	wittituralli	wididhurali	*you all spear*
	3	wittitardna	wididhardna	*they spear*

5.2 3rd Singular ergative agreement

As we have seen, Thura-Yura short-form endings work by attaching an abbreviated shape of a (usually subject) pronoun to the end of a verb. The base or root of the Thura-Yura 3rd singular pronoun is *pa-/ba-*, as seen in the 3rd singular nominative shape *banha*, and in the 3rd singular ergative shape *badlu*. Adnyamathanha has lightened or lenited the shape *pa-* to *va-* in *vanha* 'he, she NOMINATIVE' and *vanhu* 'he, she ERGATIVE;' and Barngarla seems to have further lightened it to *-wu*, a shape it puts on the ends of intransitive verbs with 3rd singular subjects, again as we have seen. If the subject pronoun shape attached to the end of a verb may be understood to have had its initial consonant removed, then we could expect the 3rd singular ergative short-form pronoun shape to be **-adlu*, from *badlu*. But this is not what we find; instead we find a shape that Schürmann spells *-arru*, a shape that keeps the vowels *a* and *u* from *badlu*, but has turned the *dl* sound in the middle into a rhotic. The sound *dl* is a pre-stopped apico-alveolar lateral: it is therefore likely that the rhotic that has replaced it is also an apico-alveolar sound. This leaves us with either the tap *r* or the trill *rr*. I would opt for the tap sound *r*, as represented above, as this sound is probably closer to the original consonant *dl* than is the trill: but again, this is only a guess. Luise Hercus has also cautiously noted Kuyani *withimiru* 'they would spear (?)' and *withiniru* 'for spearing (?)' (2006a), as well as *withini-ru* 'they might spear (?)' (2006c). It is just possible that one of these forms might contain the 3rd singular ergative subject shape of this verb.

5.3 Past tense

In the past tense forms of this verb shown below, note how the past-tense ending that we saw as *-na* on the verb *nguga-* 'go,' has now become *-ni* to harmonize with the vowels in *widi-* 'spear.' This is seen in all forms except those with 3rd singular *-aru*, dual *-ma-*, and plural *-nha:*

		SCHÜRMANN	PHONEMIC	ENGLISH
Sg:	1	ngatto wittinni	ngadhu widini	*I speared*
	2	nunno wittinni	nhurnu widini	*you speared*
	3	padlo wittinnarru	badlu widinaru	*he or she speared*
Du:	1	ngadli wittinni	ngadli widini	*we two speared*
	2	nuwalla wittimanna	nhuwala widimana	*you two speared*
	3	pudlanbi wittimanna	budlanbi widimana	*they two speared*
Pl:	1	ngarrinyelbo wittinni	ngarinyarlbu widini	*we speared*
	2	nuralli wittinnanna	nhurali widinanha	*you all speared*
	3	yardna wittinnanna	yardna widinanha	*they speared*

		SHORT FORM	ENGLISH
Sg:	1	widinadhu	*I speared*
	2	widinurnu	*you speared*
	3	widinaru	*he or she speared*
Du:	1	widinadli	*we two speared*
	2	widinuwala	*you two speared*
	3	(widimana)	*they two speared*

Pl:	1	widinarinyarlbu	*we speared*
	2	widinurali	*you all speared*
	3	widinardna	*they speared*

5.4 Imperative

The transitive imperative forms for *widi-* 'spear' are as follows: notice how in the singular the imperative ending *-ga* harmonizes with the *i* sound of the verb root that comes before it, to make *-gi*:

Sg:	wittiki	widigi	*spear it!*
Du:	wittimakka	widimaga	*you both spear it!*
Pl:	wittikanna	widiganha	*you all spear it!*

However the imperative ending harmonizes only sporadically with a preceding vowel, as we will see; it often retains its shape *-ga* after *u*. This aspect of vowel harmony, like prestopping, appears to have been variable.

5.5 Hortative

The transitive hortative verbs, that is, those that mean, *let (someone) do (something); (someone) can or may do (something)*, are as follows. Again, the second person (you) shapes of these verbs are the same as, and probably mean much the same as the imperative forms, and have been put up into the imperative set above.

Sg:	1	witti	widi(yi)	*let me spear it, I can spear it*
	3	wittiarru	widiyaru	*let him/her spear it, he/she can spear it*
Du:	1	wittimadli	widimadli	*let's both spear it, we can both spear it*
	3	wittimai	widimayi	*let them both spear it*
Pl:	1	wittirrinyelbo	widirinyarlbu	*let's spear it, we can spear it*
	3	wittiadna	widiyardna	*let them spear it, they can spear it*

Again, these verbs seem to consist mainly of short-form pronouns attached to a bare verb root. But here we can see the sound *y* appearing in all third person shapes, and possibly in the 1st singular shape as well. The shape that Schürmann spells *wittiadna* is probably *widiyardna* with a retroflex *rd* sound, because all his other 3rd plural short forms show a retroflex stop in this position. A sentence example containing an hortative shape of the transitive verb *nhunggu-* 'give,' with vowel harmony extending into the pronoun ending, is repeated here:

(5.1)   ngai   kurrumidlantarringe   maii   nungkurdnu
(g22)   ngayi   gurrumidlandarringi   mayi   nhunggurdnu
         ngayi   gurru-midla-nda-rri-ngi   mayi   nhunggu-ardna
         I/me   stick-spr.thrwr-ASSOC-HUM.PL-ERG   food   give-3.pl

let the Adelaide people give me food

The expression *gurrumidlandarri* was the Barngarla name for the people who lived on the Adelaide plain (see Section 7.3.3).

5.6 Desiderative

The desiderative verb forms, meaning *(someone) wants to do (something)* are as follows. Again, Schürmann offers us mainly short forms:

Sg:	1	wittingatto	widingadhu	*I want to spear it*
	2	wittingunno	widingunu	*you want to spear it*
	3	wittingarru	widingaru	*he or she wants to spear it*
Du:	1	wittingadli	widingadli	*we two want to spear it*
	2	nuwalla wittimangka	nhuwala widimangga	*you two want to spear it*
	3	pudlanbi wittimangka	budlanbi widimangga	*they two want to spear it*
Pl:	1	wittinggarrinyelbo	widinggarrinyarlbu	*we want to spear it*
	2	wittingka nuralli	widingga nhurali	*you all want to spear it*

| | | 3 | wittingardna | widingardna | *they want to spear it* |

5.7 Perfect aspect

Here are the perfect-aspect forms of the verb *widi-*, with the perfect suffix *-ndya*:

		SCHÜRMANN	PHONEMIC	ENGLISH
Sg:	1	ngatto wittintya	ngadhu widindya	*I have speared it*
	2	nunno wittintya	nhurnu widindya	*you have speared it*
	3	padlo wittintyarru	badlu widindyaru	*he or she has speared it*
Du:	1	ngadli wittintya	ngadli widindya	*we have both speared it*
	2	nuwalla wittimantya	nhuwala widimandya	*you have both speared it*
	3	pudlanbi wittimantya	budlanbi widimandya	*they have both speared it*
Pl:	1	ngarrinyelbo wittintya	ngarinyarlbu widindya	*we have speared it*
	2	nuralli wittintyanna	nhurali widindyanha	*you have all speared it*
	3	yardna wittintyanna	yardna widindyanha	*they have speared it*

		SHORT FORM	ENGLISH
Sg:	1	widindyadhu	*I have speared it*
	2	widindyunu	*you have speared it*
	3	widindyaru	*he or she has speared it*
Du:	1	widindyadli	*we have both speared it*
	2	widindyuwala	*you have both speared it*
	3	(widimandya)	*they have both speared it*
Pl:	1	widindyarinyarlbu	*we have speared it*
	2	widindyurali	*you have all speared it*
	3	widindyardna	*they have speared it*

Schürmann's vocabulary gives us the following sentence showing perfect-aspect verb forms:

(5.2) (78)

ngai	yalbaintyanna	Battara	yurarringe	mundulturri
ngayi	yalbandyanha	Badharra	yurharringi,	Munduldurri
ngayi	yalba-ndya-nha	Badharra	yurha-rri-ngi	Munduldu-rri
me	hate-PERF-2,3.pl	NAME	man-HUM.PL-ERG	European-HUM.PL

yauurru	kattintyanna
yawurru	gadindyanha
yawurru	gadi-ndya-nha
at.once	bring-PERF-2,3.pl

the Badharra tribe have declared to kill me, having fetched the Europeans straight

Schürmann lists a verb *yalbadha* 'hate, destine to death,' which is found here. The shape of the last verb, *gadindyanha* with its 2,3 plural subject suffix *-nha*, shows that it is the men from the land named after the eucalypt called Badharra, and not the speaker, who have fetched the Europeans. Schürmann's *battara* is 'scrubby gum,' and Kuyani has *patharra* 'box tree' (Hercus 2006a).

5.8 Subjunctive present

The shapes for the subjunctive meaning of the transitive verb *widi-*, are as follows. Remember that these shapes mean that someone *could, might, would* or *should* do something, and have a subjunctive suffix that may appear as *-rha, -rhi* or *-rhu*, depending on the verb it is attached to:

		SCHÜRMANN	PHONEMIC	ENGLISH
Sg:	1	ngatto wittiri	ngadhu widirhi	*I might spear it*
	2	nunno wittiri	nhurnu widirhi	*you might spear it*
	3	padlo wittiru	badlu widirhu	*he or she might spear it*
Du:	1	ngadli wittiri	ngadli widirhi	*we two might spear it*
	2	nuwalla wittimara	nhuwala widimarha	*you two might spear it*

	3	pudlanbi wittimara	budlanbi widimarha	*they two might spear it*
Pl:	1	ngarrinyelbo wittiri	ngarinyarlbu widirhi	*we might spear it*
	2	nuralli wittiranna *or* wittirna	nhurali widirhanha *or* widirna	*you all might spear it*
	3	yardna wittiranna *or* wittirna	yardna widirhanha *or* widirna	*they might spear it*

		SHORT FORM	ENGLISH
Sg:	1	widirhadhu	*I might spear it*
	2	widirhunu	*you might spear it*
	3	widiru	*he or she might spear it*
Du:	1	widirhadli	*we two might spear it*
	2	widirhuwala	*you two might spear it*
	3	(widimarha)	*they two might spear it*
Pl:	1	widirharinyarlbu	*we might spear it*
	2	widirhurali	*you all might spear it*
	3	widirhardna	*they might spear it*

Notice here how the subjunctive ending that we saw as *-rha* on the verb *nguga-* 'go,' is now *-rhi*, to harmonize with the vowel in the stem of *widi-*. In the 3rd singular shape, the ending might have been *-rha-ru*, (SUBJUNCTIVE *rha* + 3rd singular ergative short form *-ru*), and indeed this is the shape we find in the 3rd singular transitive *past-tense* subjunctive form below. Instead, here the ending has been shortened to *-rhu*, taking just the first and last sounds of the shape *-rharu*. We can tell that Schürmann intended the retroflex rhotic *rh* here, and not the flap *r*, because in these lists he consistently uses the letter *r (rh)* for the subjunctive suffix, and just as consistently writes *-arru (-aru)* for the ergative short-form ending.

5.9 Subjunctive past

The past-tense subjunctive forms of the verb *widi-* are show in Table 5.1 at the end of this chapter. And there in the 3rd singular form we see the suffix spelled out, as it were, with both the subjunctive shape *-rha* and the 3rd singular ergative-subject shape *-ru* put together: *widindya<u>rharu</u>*.

The short forms of transitive past-tense subjunctive verbs may have looked like this:

		SHORT FORM	ENGLISH
Sg:	1	widindyarhadhu	*I would have speared it*
	2	widindyarhunu	*you would have speared it*
	3	widindyarharu	*he or she would have speared it*
Du:	1	widindyarhadli	*we would have both speared it*
	2	widindyarhuwala	*you would have both speared it*
	3	(widimandyarha)	*they would have both speared it*
Pl:	1	widindyarharinyarlbu	*we would have speared it*
	2	widindyarhurali	*you would have all speared it*
	3	widindyarhardna	*they would have speared it*

5.10 Pluperfect

Schürmann lists singular shapes of a tense he calls 'plus perfect,' probably pluperfect. This tense refers to the past in the past, such as in an English sentence like *I had gone*. The shapes he records are as follows:

1. wittinyanna
2. wittinyan
3. wittinyannarru

These are clearly the 1st, 2nd and 3rd singular shapes of the verb *widi-* 'spear, pierce,' with short-form pronoun suffixes. We can see the 3rd singular ergative suffix *-aru*, and a 2nd singular suffix *-n*. We cannot be sure of the shape of the 1st singular suffix. The tense ending looks like *-nya* in the 2nd singular form, and possibly *-nyanha* in the other forms. Unfortunately we cannot say much more about it than this.

		SCHÜRMANN	PHONEMIC	MEANING
Sg:	1	ngatto wittintyara	ngadhu widindyarha	*I would have speared it*
	2	nunno wittintyara	nhurnu widindyarha	*you would have speared it*
	3	padlo wittintyararru	badlu widindyarharru	*he or she would have speared it*
Dual:	1	ngadli wittintyara	ngadli widindyarha	*we would have both speared it*
	2	nuwalla wittimantyara	nhuwala widimandyarha	*you would have both speared it*
	3	pudlanbi wittimantyara	budlanbi widimandyarha	*they would have both speared it*
Plural:	1	ngarrinyelbo wittintyara	ngarinyarlbu widindyarha	*we would have speared it*
	2	nuralli wittintyaranna *or* wittintyarna	nhurali widindyarhanha *or* widindyarna	*you would have all speared it*
	3	yardna wittintyaranna *or* wittintyarna	yardna widindyarhanha *or* widindyarna	*they would have speared it*

Table 5.1: Subjunctive past forms of *widi-* 'spear'

Six: Harry Crawford's Barngarla verbs

Among the words and phrases that Harry Crawford provided to Ken Hale at Iron Knob in 1960 were a set of verbs (O'Grady 2001). These verb forms provide a useful check on some of Schürmann's material.

Crawford's responses give evidence of a phonological rule in Northern Barngarla that lenites *g* to *w* between two *u* vowels:

velar lenition: g → w / u __ u

Crawford's verbs are as follows:

1	Imperatives:	nhakuka	*see*
2		nyungkuwu	*give*
3	Presents:	yuruwuthu	*hear*
4		ngalkuthu	*eat*
5		kawu yapatha	*drink water*
6		wangkatha	*speak*
7		ikatha	*sit*
8		ukatha	*walk, go*
9		pardni ngukatha	*return*
10		miya warnithi	*sleep*
11	Wirangu presents:	ngarna walarin	*run*

12		karra warnikin	*climb*
13		nyirlinyin	*cry (weep)*
14	Pasts:	padlunu	*died*
15		pirdnanha	*hit with hand*
16		nganhay warninhi ~ wardninhi	*child fell from tree*

All the following references are to Schürmann's vocabulary (Schürmann 1844).

(1) The form *nakkuttu* 'see, understand, know' is phonemic *nhagudhu*. Note here that the imperative suffix *-ga* does not harmonize with the proceeding vowel *u* in this instance, to make a shape **nhagugu (→*nhaguwu)*.

(2) The verb 'give' in Thura-Yura languages is either *nhunggV-* or *yunggV-*; Crawford's *nyungku-* appears to be a Northern Barngarla variant. Schürmann has *nhungguga* for the imperative of *nhunggu-* 'give' (see sentence example (7.15a) in Section 7.5.1), although it is clear from his verb paradigms that the imperative suffix *-ga* could elsewhere harmonize with a preceding vowel. This would yield an expected imperative shape *nyunggugu** in Northern Barngarla, which by velar lenition would yield attested *nyungkuwu*.

(3-10) Note vowel harmony in present-tense suffixes

(3) *yurrukkutu* 'hear' is phonemic *yurhugudhu*, then with velar lenition *yurhuwudhu* at Iron Knob.

(4) *ngalgutu* 'to eat,' phonemic *ngalgudhu*.

(5) *kauo* 'water,' phonemic *gawu*. Elsewhere in Crawford's list 'water' is *kawi*. *yappata* 'suck, drink,' is phonemic *yabadha*.

(8) *ngugadha* 'walk, go.'

(9) *pardni* 'hither, this way.'

(10) *meya* 'sleep,' phonemic *miya; worniti* 'to fall,' phonemic *warnidhi*.

(11-13) Note the Wirangu present-tense ending *-n*.

(14) *badlutu* 'die,' phonemic *badludhu*. Crawford's word here confirms the apico-alveolar shape of the nasal in the past-tense suffix.

(15) O'Grady finds no correspondence for this word in Schürmann, when in fact there is: *pitata* 'knock, pelt, stamp, kick,' phonemic *pirdadha* (cf Kuyani *pirda-* 'hit against something'). Schürmann's sentence example is:

(6.1) kauunga   pitatarru

(58)   gawunga   pirdadharu

        gawu-nga   pirda-dha-aru

        water-ERG   hit-PRES-3.sg.ERG

the rain is pelting

The shape Hale heard as *pirdnanha* is most likely:

(6.2) pirdananha

pirda-na-nha

hit-PAST-2,3.pl

(you pl/ they) hit

(16) *nganhay* is almost certainly a variant on the interrogative/indefinite demonstrative *nganha* 'who, what/somebody' (see Section 9.3). The verb root is *warni-* and prestopped variant *wardni-* 'fall' (qv). The difficulty is the apparent past-tense ending *-nhi*, which should by the reasoning set out above be *-ni*. The past-tense allomorph may have been laminalized before *i*: so *-na, -nu, -nhi*: but on the evidence of a single attestation from a lapsed speaker this must remain a possibility only.

Seven: Suffixes on nouns

For lots of the meanings that English conveys by way of prepositions like *to, from, over, under, after* and so on, Barngarla uses suffixes. Schürmann provides us with a number of important shapes that are suffixed to nouns, to make meanings for which English uses prepositions.

7.1 Markedness

Across Australia a suffix *-nya* or *-nha* is widely used to mark something as being in some way different or special. The Thura-Yura languages are the same; the suffix *-nha* has a wide range of uses here too. Luise Hercus describes this suffix in Kuyani as:

> [a] nominal clitic with multiple functions: it can be a proper noun marker and is therefore common in placenames ... it is used to 'single out' or particularise adjectives and is especially common in possessive adjectives ... sometimes also affixed to adverbs ... sometimes it is just emphatic (Hercus 2006a)

This suffix is ubiquitous as well in Adnyamathanha, so much so that Tunstill (2004: 434) can say of it only that it is 'of uncertain/variable meaning,' and Schebeck (1974: 4) says that it is 'doubtlessly the most difficult to define.' Because of the ubiquity of this suffix in all Thura-Yura languages, where Schürmann has an ending *-nna* or *-na,* and where I am unable to find a context for such an ending in another language, I will cautiously and rather reluctantly assume that this shape could be phonemic *-nha,* and proceed as if it were.

7.2 Plural & dual

In Australia as elsewhere, it is frequently the case that only human nouns, or nouns that refer to highly animate things, may take marking for non-singular number (dual or plural); usually men, women, dogs and/or children.[11] Schürmann has the following, repeated here with suggested phonemic representations:

SCHÜRMANN	PHONEMIC	ENGLISH
yurra	yurha	*man*
yurralbelli	yurhalbili	*two men*
yurrarri	yurharri	*men*
pallara	barlarha	*woman*
pallalbelli	barlalbili	*two women*
pallarri	barlarri	*women*

Both Adnyamathanha and Kuyani show two forms of the dual-marking suffix, *-alypila* and *-alpila* (Hercus 2006, Tunstill 2004: 428). Schürmann spells the Barngarla equivalent *-lbelli*, without indication of fronting and raising of a preceding vowel: so, *yurralbelli* and *pallalbelli*, not ˣ*yurrailbelli* or ˣ*pallailbelli*. This makes the shape of the Barngarla suffix as *-lbili*, certain. Schürmann says that this suffix is an abbreviation of the number *kalbelli* 'two,' which is phonemic *galbili*. Nhukunu has *paarla* 'woman' (Hercus 1992: 26), and I will presume that the rhotic in the Barngarla word copies the place of articulation (retroflex) of the preceding lateral consonant.

Human body parts usually come in pairs, and nouns for these could be marked for dual number in Barngarla. In Schürmann's vocabulary we can see the following:

---

[11] The widespread distinction between nouns that refer to highly animate entities, and those which do not, is most frequently discussed in the context of case-marking. The definitive but rather technical explanation of this phenomenon is Silverstein (1976), with a more accessible discussion appearing in Garrett (1990: 261-262). Another example of pluralization being confined to highly animate nouns in an Australian language may be seen in Clendon (2014: 94-96).

pinkalbelli	birngalbili	*two hips*
marralbelli	marhalbili	*two hands*

We have no analogue for the Barngarla plural shape that Schürman spells *-rri*. However the trill *rr* is widely used in Australia to mark plurality: its acoustic shape as a series of taps against the alveolar ridge makes it iconic of plurality. Indeed, and as Dixon (2002: 253-256) points out, in Australia the number suffix *-rrV* nearly always marks plurality of some sort. Of the three rhotic sounds available in Barngarla, therefore, the trilled shape *-rri* seems to be the most likely as a marker of plurality on human nouns.

A suffix Schürmann spells *-ilyaranna* signals 'a great number or quantity.' Wirangu has two plural-marking suffixes with very specific applications, *-ilya* and *-ra* (Miller et al 2010: 49, 75), and it may be that the Barngarla shape is composed of these: *-lya-ra-nha* → *-lyaranha*. It is likely to be the case that the lamino-palatal lateral *ly* fronts the vowel *u* to phonetic [y] when it comes in front of this suffix. Schürmann offers the following, based on the nouns *yurha* 'man, person' and *gawu* 'water:'

SCHÜRMANN:	yurrailyaranna	kauülyaranna
PHONEMIC:	yurhalyaranha	gawulyaranha
TRANSLATION:	*a great number of people*	*a great quantity of water*

7.3 Ergative & locative

Another suffix with a number of uses in Barngarla is the ending *-ngV*. This ending may (or may not) harmonize with a preceeding vowel.

7.3.1 Ergative *-ngV*

The suffix *-nga* marks a noun as being the subject of a transitive verb: it is the *ergative* case-suffix on nouns, but does not occur on pronouns. Note that most singular pronouns have their own dedicated ergative shapes: *ngadhu* 'I,' *nhurnu* 'you,' and *badlu* 'he, she.' Schürmann offers us the following transitive sentences to show how this suffix is used, where the subject of the first sentence is someone's name, Tyilkelli:

(7.1a) Tyilkellinga ngai kúndanarru
(g4) Dyilgilinga ngayi gurndanaru
Dyilgili-nga ngayi gurnda-na-aru
NAME-ERG I.NOM hit-PAST-3.sg.ERG

Tyilkili me did beat

(7.1b) kutyu yurarringe iratanna
(7) gudyu yurharringi irradhanha
gudyu yurha-rri-ngi irra-dha-nha
other man-HUM.PL-ERG keep.off-PRES-2,3.pl

the other men keep us off

(7.1c) ngarrungu wittitanna ngarrinyelbo
(47) ngarrungu wididhanha ngarinyarlbu
ngarru-ngu widi-dha-nha ngarinyarlbu
surround-ERG spear-PRES-2,3.pl we/us

they will surround and spear us

Hercus (2006a) has *kurnda-* 'hit, kill' for Kuyani; Miller et al (2010: 46) have *gurndarn* 'hit' in Wirangu, and McEntee & McKenzie (1992: 27) have *urnda-* 'kill' in Adnyamathanha. Kuyani also has *kutyu* 'other, different' (Hercus 2006a). Schürmann records *irata* 'keep off, defend, protect,' while Adnyamathanha has *irra-ngu-* 'protect, defend' (with applicative suffix *-ngu*, see Section 10.8) (McEntee & McKenzie 1992: 22). Schürmann has an apparent adverb *ngarru* 'circle, enclosure,' which may correspond to the Kuyani verb *ngawu-* 'round up, encircle' (Hercus 2006a), and to Adnyamathanha *ngarr-arhu* 'cornered, bailed up' (McEntee & McKenzie 1992: 41). The Barngarla word *ngarru* is probably an adverb marked for ergative case in agreement with the predicate's transitive subject, as '(they) encircling ... .' This kind of syntax is reasonably common in Australia.[12]

Nouns marked for dual number may also take ergative case-marking:

(7.2)   maii   kaltanyilbellinge   ngai   yeringumatta

(11)   mayi   garldanyilbilingi   ngayi   yaringumadha

         mayi   garldanyi-lbili-ngi   ngayi   yari-ngu-ma-dha

         food   begging-DU-ERG   I/me   greedy-APPL-2,3.du-PRES

the two beggars ask me for food

Adnyamathanha has *arlda-* 'call out' (McEntee & McKenzie 1992: 14), which I will take to correspond in part to Schürmann's adjective *kaltanye/garldanyi* 'begging'. Schürmann's vocabulary has a derived verb *garldiridhi* 'be clamorous, beg,' with a root *garldi/a-* which must have roughly the same meaning: its similarity to *garla-* 'call out' is noted again in Section 10.8.2. The ending *-nyi* seen here forming an adjective looks like a gerundive ending, although it is not noted in Schürmann's grammar along with other non-finite verb forms (see Section 11.2). Be that as it may, it appears to enable the root *garldi-* to accept nominal inflections for number and case, and to serve thus as a substantive adjective. Also in this sentence we see the adjective *yari* 'greedy' with an applicative suffix (see Section 10.8), used to create a transitive verb with two objects: the thing desired (food), and its source (me). This derived verb now has a meaning something like 'crave, require [OBJECT 1] from [OBJECT 2].' The applicative derivation of the adjective *yari* 'greedy' is noted again in Section 10.8.2.

7.3.2 Instrumental *-ngV, -nda*

This ending marks something as being an instrument: in effect, some inanimate object or tool that is used to accomplish some action. Schürmann offers us the following sentence, with *ganya* 'stone' being used as an instrument:

---

[12] For example, time and manner adverbs in Warlpiri are inflected for ergative case when occurring in transitive clauses (Hale 1982: 279-281).

(7.3)	Marrályinga	ngai	píttanarrù	kányanga
(g5)	marralyinga	ngayi	birdanaru	ganyanga
	marralyi-nga	ngayi	birda-na-aru	ganya-nga
	boy-ERG	I/me	hit/pelt-PAST-3.sg.ERG	stone-INST

The boy me did hit with a stone

Notice here how both the subject *(marralyi* 'boy') and the instrument *(ganya* 'stone') get marked by *-nga:* ergative and instrumental —human and non-human — in each case. This double or polysemous use of a single suffix for both ergative and instrumental is common in Australian languages (see, eg, Dixon 2002: 165-166).

Hercus (2006a) has *pirda-* 'hit against something,' in Kuyani, with a sentence example 'a stone might hit us,' and McEntee & McKenzie (1992: 64) for Adnyamathanha have *virta-* 'hammer away on.' Hercus (2006a) has *kadnya* 'stone' in Kuyani, McEntee & McKenzie 1992: 2 have *adnya* 'stone' in Adnyamathanha, and Nhukunu has *katnya* (Hercus 1992: 20).

I have not been able to find the word *marralyi* 'boy' in another Thura-Yura language. Schebeck (1973: 27, 42) lists the Adnyamathanha birth-order name *marra-anha* for a fourth-born child if male, spelled *marr-anha* by McEntee & McKenzie (1992: 81). Although this is different from the Barngarla equivalent given by Schürmann *(munni),* it may contain a root that was used for 'boy' more generally in Barngarla, so I will assume that the rhotic in Schürmann's transcription is a trill: *marralyi*. Schürmann spells this word *marralye* in his vocabulary, in the phrase *purro marralye* 'still a boy,' under the lemma *purro* 'still, yet.' He also has an entry *marralye* 'fiend, devil.' In this word his *e* could be phonemic *a* after lamino-palatal *ly* as suggested in Section 2.1.1: *marralya;* and/or the rhotic could be different (either a flap or a glide).

As in English, an instrument may be an abstract entity, or it may constitute a metaphorical expression, as is seen in the following:

(7.4) Pidnyu   madlanga   wanggata
(56) Bidnyu   madlanga   wanggadha
      Bidnyu   madla-nga   wangga-dha
      shame   no-INST   speak-PRES

   He speaks with no shame

Here a certain way of expressing oneself is described by means of an instrumental metaphor.

Schürmann has another instrumental suffix, *-nta* (possibly phonemic *-nda*), without correspondence in contemporary Thura-Yura languages. The example he gives is:

(7.5) midlanta   wittiti
(g7) midlanda   wididhi
      midla-nda   widi-dhi
      spear.thrower-INST   pierce-PRES

   throw [spears] with the wommara

Midla 'spearthrower' is a common Thura-Yura word (cf eg Adnyamathanha: McEntee & McKenzie 1992: 84, Kaurna: Amery & Simpson 2013: 220). We may never know how the meanings of the instrumental suffixes *-nga* and *-nda* were different, or even if they were different.

7.3.3 Adelaide people

Schürmann records the name *Gurrumidlanda* for people who lived on the Adelaide Plain. This name is constructed as follows:

(7.6) gurrumidlanda

   gurru-midla-nda

   stick-spear.thrower-INST/ASSOC

   (people) with/ having narrow spear-throwers

This is probably an exonym: it is not recorded near Adelaide itself. Barngarla *gurru* is 'stick,' and may describe the kind of spear-throwers Adelaide people used. The phrase *gurru midla* might refer to a narrow, stick-like spear-thrower, which may have characterized Adelaide people from the point of view of people who used broader implements, although Adelaide spear-throwers do not appear to have been especially narrow (from contemporary illustrations as shown in eg. Hylton 2012: 84). It is unlikely that *gurru* is being used here as a noun classifier: this would only be to label Adelaide people as '(people) with CLASSIFIER spear-throwers,' in a culture where everyone used spearthrowers.

The morpheme *-nda* is almost certainly the instrumental suffix, and gives evidence of a conflation of instrumental and associative meanings (cf. English *hit it with the hammer* (instrumental), versus. *put it in the box with the hammer* (associative). The suffix *-nda* is not recorded with any word other than *midla;* it may have been specific to that noun: the usual instrumental suffix is *-ngV*, and the usual associative suffix is *-lyga*. Schürmann records the following use of this term:

(7.7) (21)

Nantinge	kurrumidlantarri	ngalla	kuputarru
Nandingi	gurrumidlandarri	ngarla	gubudharu
Nandi-ngi	gurru-midla-nda-rri	ngarla	gubu-dha-aru
NAME-ERG	stick-sp.thrwr-INST-HUM.PL	many	represent-PRES-3.sg.ERG

Nanti represents the Adelaide natives as very numerous

Schürmann records *gubudhu* 'state, maintain, represent with vehement gesture.'

7.3.4 Locative *-ngV*

This meaning indicates that something is on, at, by, in or near something else: something is located next to or close to something else. Schürmann offers *wortannanga* 'in the sea,' which could be *wardarnanga*. Schürmann has *wortanna* 'sea;' and Wirangu has *warna* (Miller et al 2010: 84), which is reminiscent of the Barngarla word. He also offers *garngunga* 'in the house;' Schürmann has *karnko* 'hut, house, place of encampment.' Adnyamathanha has *arnku* 'camp' (McEntee & McKenzie 1992: 6), and Kuyani has *kanku* 'house' (Hercus 2006a), without retroflexion, in the sentence *wiltyalangka thitari ngalpaaku ngatyunhangka kankungka* 'last night some children got into my house.'

Other locative expressions in Schürmann's vocabulary are:

(7.8a)　　kapmarra　　innaityinge　　ikkat ai
(14)　　　gabmarra　　inhadyingi　　igadhayi
　　　　　gabmarra　　inha-dyi-ngi　　iga-dha-ayi
　　　　　always　　　this-TOP-LOC　　sit-PRES-1.sg.NOM
　　　　　I shall always live here

(7.8b)　　parungu　　karitanna　　yurarri
(15)　　　barhungu　　garhidhanha　　yurharri
　　　　　barhu-ngu　　garhi-dha-nha　　yurha-rri
　　　　　game-LOC　　be-PRES-2,3.pl　　man-HUM.PL
　　　　　the men are still at the game, are hunting still

(7.8c)　　Nillinge　　pappi　　ngaitye　　ikkatao
(39)　　　Nhirlingi　　babi　　ngadyi　　igadhawu
　　　　　nhirli-ngi　　babi　　ngadyi　　iga-dha-wu
　　　　　sorrow-LOC　　father　　my　　sit-PRES-3.sg.NOM
　　　　　My father is in sorrow

The use and meanings of the existential intransitive verbs *iga-* and *garhi-* are addressed in Section 12.3. Again and as in English, the locative suffix can be used for abstract or metaphorical expressions as seen in (7.8b) and (7.8c). Performing a certain activity (hunting) is denoted by means of a locative metaphor, and the expression of a certain emotional state (sorrow) also employs a locative metaphor.

7.3.5 Subordinating -nga

The suffix -nga is also used to mark clauses that state the background or reason for some event or action that happens in the main clause. Schürmann offers two Barngarla sentences that have clauses marked in this way. In these examples the background clauses are set off within square brackets:

(7.9) (g5)

Panna	ngultapanga	mundulturri	babmantinanna
banha	nguldabanga,	munduldurri	babmandinanha
[banha	nguldaba-nga]	munduldu-rri	babmandi-na-nha
[he	young.man-LOC]	european-HUM.PL	come/return-PAST-2,3.pl

[When he (was) a young man], the Europeans arrived

Schürmann has *ngultapa* 'young man.' Teichelmann (1857: 43) has *ngulta* 'the cuts on the back & chest of the *wilyuru*', and as the *wilyarhu* was an initiation ceremony, Barngarla *ngultapa/nguldaba* may have referred to a young man recently initiated. The word *mundulturri* clearly shows the human plural suffix *-rri* attached to *mundultu/munduldu* 'European.' Schürmann has *babmantiti* 'come, return,' which must be phonemic *babmandidhi*, with present-tense ending *-dhi*. Adnyamathanha has *vabma-* 'grow, rise, come up, emerge' (McEntee & McKenzie 1992: 58), and Kuyani has *papmanta* 'break open' (Hercus 2006c). These words convey metaphorically the semantics of emerging and appearing, and the Kuyani form confirms the shape of the *-nt-/-nd-* cluster in the verb *babma<u>nd</u>inanha* 'they appeared/arrived.'

This sentence is made up of two parts or clauses: *banha nguldabanga* 'as a young man,' and *munduldurri babmandinanha* 'Europeans arrived/appeared.' The first clause gets a locative *-nga* suffix because it sets the scene and timing for the event in the main clause, the arrival of Europeans.

The second sentence of this sort that Schürmann offers is:

(7.10) ngukatia   maii   madlanga
(g5)   ngugadhiya   mayi   madlanga
       nguga-dha-iya   [mayi   madla-nga]
       go-PRES-1.sg.NOM [food   none-LOC]

I shall go away [because I have no food]

Teichelmann (1857: 21) has *madla* 'merely' in Kaurna; Kuyani has *madla* meaning 'no, nothing' (Hercus 2006a), and Schürmann has *madla* 'no, none.' This is another sentence made up of two clauses. The main clause tells us what the speaker is going to do: *ngugadhiya* 'I'm going away:' The second clause, marked with locative *-nga*, tells us the background or reason for his going away: *mayi madlanga* '(because of) no food.'

7.4 Possessive, allative & purposive

The suffix *-rhu* also has a number of uses in Barngarla:

7.4.1 Possessive *-rhu*

The suffix *-rhu* may mark possession or ownership in Barngarla. In the following sentence you can see this suffix permanently attached to the interrogative possessive pronoun *nganhkurhu* 'whose?', as well as being suffixed to the name Wingalta:

(7.11) inna   ngankuru   palta?   Wingaltaru
(g5)   inha   nganhkurhu baldha?   Wingaldarhu
       inha   nganhkurhu baldha   wingalda-rhu
       this   whose   cloak   NAME-POSS

Whose cloak is this? Wingalta's

Wirangu has *baldha* 'skin cloak' (Miller et al 2010: 3) and *inha* 'this' (Hercus 1999: 64). Kuyani and Adnyamathanha have *nganha* 'who?' and Kuyani has *nganharhu* 'whose?' (Hercus 2006a).

7.4.2 Allative -*rhu*

In this use, -*rhu* marks direction towards whatever noun or pronoun it is attached to, as the following sentence shows:

(7.12)   ngai   ngukata   karnkuru
(g5)   ngayi   ngugadha   garngurhu
        ngayi   nguga-dha   garngu-rhu
        I   go-PRES   house-ALL

I shall go home

7.4.3 Purposive -*rhu*

This suffix can be used to mark something as a goal or a purpose; an end for which someone is aiming. Schürmann offers the following sentences to illustrate this usage:

(7.13)   kalalta   mankut'atto   kuyaru
(g5)   garlalda   mankudhadhu   guyarhu
        garlalda   manku-dha-adhu   guya-rhu
        torch   take-PRES-1.sg.ERG   fish-PURP

I shall take dry bark to fish

Schürmann has *mankutu* 'take, receive,' which is phonemic *mankudhu*. Schürmann, as well as Miller et al (2010: 46) for Wirangu have *kuya/guya* 'fish.' Schürmann's *kalalta* is 'torch, dry bark lighted and used in fishing at night.' I cannot find another Thura-Yura word corresponding to *kalalta*, although Wirangu has *garla* 'fire' (Miller et al 2010: 37), and Kuyani has the prestopped variant *kardla* (Hercus 2006a); O'Grady 2001 also has *kardla* for 'fire.' I suspect that 'fire' may be a part of Schürmann's *kalalta*, and that he may not have recognized this, as he has *gadla* for 'fire,' with different spelling, and with prestopping.

(7.14)	maiiru	ngukatai
(g5)	mayirhu	ngugadhayi
	mayi-rhu	nguga-dha-ayi
	food-PURP	go-PRES-1.sg.NOM

I shall go for food

Note also the shape *nganharhu*, 'what for? why?' with the purposive suffix *-rhu*, as may be seen in sentence example (7.18b) in Section 7.5.4, and in Section 9.3.

7.5 Other grammatical suffixes

Schürmann lists 22 other suffixes that go on nouns, with a brief discussion of each. Those words of Schürmann's that I am unable to locate in modern Thura-Yura texts, I will leave much the same as Schürmann wrote them.

7.5.1 Dative *-ni*

Schürmann says that this suffix is 'of an entreating nature,' and that it 'may perhaps denote the dative case.' This is almost certainly so, as both his examples employ the verb *nhunggu-* 'give.' Kaurna also has *-ni* marking the dative case (Amery & Simpson 2013: 121).

(7.15a)	ngai inni,	ngai inni	nungkuka	pappi
(g7)	ngayini,	ngayini	nhungguga,	babi
	ngayi-ni	ngayi-ni	nhunggu-ga	babi
	I-DAT	I-DAT	give-IMP	father

to me, to me give (it) father

(7.15b)	innanni	nungkukka,	innanni
(g7)	inhani	nhungguga,	inhani
	inha-ni	nhunggu-ga	inha-ni
	this-DAT	give-IMP	this-DAT

give it to this person, to this

Schürmann states that 'the accusative and dative are identical with the simple nominative.' The dative suffix *-ni,* therefore, was probably used for disambiguation, and/or for other discourse strategies.

7.5.2 Ablative *-ngurni*

In Chapter Three we looked at the use of the ending *-dni* or *-rdni* to mark ablative meaning on pronouns; that is, motion or direction away from someone. In Section 8.3 we will see how this suffix is used on other parts of speech. In the meanwhile, the suffix used on nouns to code a strictly ablative meaning appears to have been *-ngurni* (Schürmann's *ngunne,* cf Wirangu and Adnyamathanha *-ngurni:* Hercus 1999: 52, Tunstill 2004: 428, Schebeck 1974: 7-8), as seen in the following examples:

(7.16a)	karnko ngunne
(g6)	garngungurni
	garngu-ngurni
	house-ABL

from the house

(7.16b)	warra ngunne
(g6)	warrangurni
	warra-ngurni
	far-ABL

from far away

(7.16c) wingunne
(73) wiyingurni
wiyi-ngurni
this.moment-ABL
from now, from this instant

Schürmann has *warra* for 'out, far away, absent.' I have been unable to find a corresponding word in a contemporary Thura-Yura language, and so have left his spelling as it is. Adnyamathanha and Kuyani have an interjection *wiyi* meaning 'yes; well!' that is probably unrelated to the Barngarla word.

7.5.3 Comitative *-dninga, -rdningi*

Comitative meaning involves *accompaniment*. In Barngarla the suffixes *-dninga* and *-rdningi* are used with proper nouns (the names of people) and with pronouns (that also refer to people) to indicate that someone is in the company of someone else:

(7.17a) Yutalta yarridninga
(g6) Yudalda Yarridninga
Yudalda Yarri-dninga
NAME NAME-COM
Yudalda is with Yarri

(7.17b) kapmarra nunkurdninga ikkat'ai
(g6) gabmarra nhunkurdninga igadhayi
gabmarra nhunku-rdninga iga-dha-ayi
always 2.sg.stem.1-COM sit-PRES-1.sg.NOM
always with thee I shall stop

Schürmann has *kapmarra* 'only, always' and *ikkata* 'sit, dwell, live;' and O'Grady (2001) has *ikatha* 'sit.' Adnyamathanha also has *ika-* 'to sit, stay, remain' (McEntee & McKenzie 1992: 17). The commitative suffix is here attached to the possessive form of the pronoun, as noted in Section 3.2 above.

7.5.4 Allative *-dnurhu, -rdnurhu*

We have seen above the allative (towards something) marker *-dnirhu* on pronouns: on nouns it has a slightly different shape, as *-dnurhu* or *-rdnurhu*. It can only be used on proper nouns and pronouns:

(7.18a)	Mulyadnuru	ngukat'ai
(g6)	Mulyadnurhu	ngugadhayi
	Mulya-dnurhu	nguga-dha-ayi
	name-ALL	go-PRES-1.sg.NOM

I shall go to Mulya

(7.18b)	ngaityidnuru	ninna	ngannaru	kutta	babmantini?
(g6)	ngadyidnurhu	nhina	nganharhu	guda	babmandini?
	ngadyi-dnurhu	nhina	nganha-rhu	guda	babmandi-ni
	1.sg.stem.1-ALL	you	what-PURP	NEG	arrive-PAST

Why did you not come to me?

Above we saw the verb *babmandi-* 'emerge, appear, arrive:' here it has a past-tense marker *-ni* after the *i*-sound at the end of this verb. We saw the pronoun *ngadyidnurhu* 'to me' pronounced *ngadyidnirhu* in Section 3.1.1 above; it could probably be said either way. Kuyani and Adnyamathanha have the question-word stem *nganha-* (Hercus 2006a, McEntee & McKenzie 1992: 38), and Wirangu and Adnyamathanha have the negator *guda* (Miller et al 2010: 40, Schebeck 1974: 41 as *uta*, with loss of initial consonant).

Allative meaning may take on a metaphorical sense as well, having to do with desire or aim at a particular goal, which may not be a goal in spatial terms:

(7.19)	yura	kalkaritao		pallaradnuru
(11)	yurha	galgaridhawu		barlarhadnurhu
	yurha	galga-ri-dha-wu		barlarha-dnurhu
	man	tremble/desire-VBLZR-PRES-3.sg.NOM		woman-ALL

a man feels desire for a woman

7.5.5 Perlative *-dhari, -ngVnV*

Perlative means going by, along, or through a place. Kaurna has a perlative suffix *-tarra* (Amery & Simpson 2013: 122), similar to the Barngarla ending. Against this, Adnyamathanha has an allative suffix *-thari* (Schebeck 1974: 7), similar in meaning and quite possibly with the same shape as the Barngarla suffix:

(7.20a)	tallallatarri	ngukat'arrinyelbo
(g6)	Dhalaladhari	ngugadharinyarlbu
	Dhalala-dhari	nguga-dha-arinyarlbu
	PLACE-PERL	go-PRES-1.pl

by way of Dalala we shall go

(7.20b)	yarto	yuwatao	yurre,	mudla tarri
(g6)	yardu	yuwadhawu	yurri,	mudlhadhari
	yardu	yuwa-dha-wu	yurri	mudlha-dhari
	yonder	stand-PRES-3.sg.NOM	hill	nose-PERL

yonder stands the hill over the point

Kuyani has *yuwa-* 'stand' and *mudlha* 'nose' (Hercus 2006a). Schürmann has *mudla* 'nose, point of land:' a word for *nose* is often used to refer to a point of something in Australian languages. While Schürmann has *yurre* 'ear' corresponding to Kaurna and Kuyani *yurhi* 'ear,' Adnyamathanha has *yurru* 'range of hills' (McEntee & McKenzie 1992: 105), close to the meaning required here. Schürmann has *yartu* 'there, that one.' Wirangu has an archaic location nominal *nhardu* (Hercus 1999: 64), that may correspond to Barngarla *yardu* 'yonder.'

Schürmann lists another perlative suffux, *-nganna*, *-nginni* or *-ngunnu*, with the vowels subject to harmony with a preceding vowel. I have been unable to find a correspondence for this suffix in another Thura-Yura language, and will take the simplest option for the second nasal phoneme, as *n*. The shape of this suffix is therefore *-ngVnV*, with V standing in for its harmonizing vowels. Schürmann's examples are:

(7.21a) kaityarri widlanganna mankukka
(g8) gadyarri widlangana mankuga
       gadya-rri widla-ngana manku-ga
       child-HUM.PL path-PERL take-IMP

take the children along the path

(7.21b) wambiringinni ngukatia
(g8) wambiringini ngugadhiya
       wambiri-ngini nguga-dha-iya
       coast-PERL go-PRES-1.sg.NOM

along the coast I shall go

I have been unable to find correspondences in contemporary Thura-Yura languages for Schürmann's *kaityarri* 'children,' *widla* 'path' or *wambiri* 'coast,' and so have left these last two as he wrote them. However *kaityarri* clearly contains the human plural suffix *-rri*, leaving a shape *kaitya/gadya* 'small, little; infant, child,' which is the same as the Western Desert word *kaja* 'son,' and the Old Wangkatha or Mantjintja word *katha* 'child' (Clendon 2011).

7.5.6 Directional suffixes

Schürmann shows a directional suffix *-mba*, and another *-dla/-dli/-dlu*, in harmony with a preceeding vowel. These are illustrated attached to words that indicate compass directions. Adnyamathanha has *-dla* (without vowel harmony) in this function (McEntee & McKenzie 1992: 7). The following expressions employ Barngarla terms for 'the bearings of their peninsular country:'

(7.22) kayallamba wailbimba
(g6-7) gayala*mba* walybi*mba*
       northward *westward*

iatadla	wortattidli
yada<u>dla</u>	wardadhi<u>dli</u>
north-eastward	*south-eastward*

The Thura-Yura languages show no common word for 'north:' Schürmann's *kay-alla* is most like the Western Desert word *kayili* 'north,' although the Western Desert borrowing in Wirangu, the Thura-Yura language closest to and most influenced by the Western Desert Language, is *alindhara* 'north' (Miller et al 2010: 1). Adnyamathanha has *walypi* 'name of group, Blinman-Wilpena area;' *walypi wari* 'south west wind' (McEntee & McKenzie 1992: 116), and *wari* 'wind (old word)' (McEntee & McKenzie 1992: 114). Adnyamathanha *walypi* is thus clearly 'west' or 'southwest.' I have been unable to find any Thura-Yura correspondences for Schürmann's *iä ta* 'north east country or coast.' Adnyamathanha has *wartathirnka* 'south' (McEntee & McKenzie 1992: 108), clearly related to the Barngarla word Schürmann uses here.

Another use of the word *iä ta/iata/yada* 'north-eastern coast' is shown below, this time with the directional suffix *-mba* attached:

(7.23) (75)

Palta	wondakkaintyanna	wortannaru	ngukananna
baldha	wandhagandyanha,	wardarnarhu	ngugananha
baldha	wandhaga-ndya-nha	wardarna-rhu	nguga-na-nha
cloak	leave.behind-PERF-2,3.pl	sea-PURP	go-PAST-2,3.pl

iatamba

yadamba

yada-mba

north.east-DIR

They have left their cloaks behind, they went northeast to the sea.

As Schürmann has left us no translation of this sentence, I have provided one. Kuyani has a verb *wantha-* 'leave behind' (Hercus 2006a). For comment on the Barngarla form *wandhaga-*, see Section 4.1.1.

7.5.7 Reciprocal *-bingi*

This suffix, which Schürmann spells *-pengi*, most likely indicates reciprocality, that is, something given in return for something else. I have been unable to find correspondences for this suffix in contemporary or recently-spoken Thura-Yura languages. Schürmann records:

(7.24) gadla pengi mai nungkunanna

(g7) gardlabingi mayi nhunggunanha

gardla-bingi mayi nhunggu-na-nha

fire-RECIP food give-PAST-2,3.pl

for fire wood they gave the food

Most Thura-Yura languages have *yungku-* for 'give' (eg Kaurna: Amery & Simpson 2013: 125; Kuyani: Hercus 2006a, Nhukunu: Hercus 1992: 34 *(yungka-))*. However Adnyamathanha has *nhungku-* 'give' (McEntee & McKenzie 1992: 53), and Hercus (2006a) has one attestation of *nhungku-* as well, in the sentence *Alice Oldfield ngawarla nhungkuta* 'this is the language that Alice Oldfield gives (you).'

7.5.8 Avoidance *-yalani*

I have been unable to find correspondences for this shape in contemporary or recently-spoken Thura-Yura languages. This suffix, which Schürmann spells *-yallani*, appears to mark something as being an unfortunate cause of something else, perhaps corresponding to the Western Desert avoidance suffix *-ngkamarra* in this usage, in the sentence Schürmann offers below:

(7.25)	warru yallani	paitya	ngutarritanna
(g7)	waruyalani	badya	ngudharidhanha
	waru-yalani	badya	ngudha-ri-dha-nha
	kangaroo-AVOID	angry	do/argue-VBLZR-PRES-2,3.pl

about a kangaroo they quarrel

Wirangu has *waru* 'grey kangaroo' (Miller et al 2010: 85). Adnyamathanha has *vatya* 'savage, cross' (McEntee & McKenzie 1992: 55), and Kuyani has *patya* 'rage, furious anger' (Hercus 2006a). Both Adnyamathanha and Kuyani have a verb *ngutha-* 'make, do' (McEntee & McKenzie 1992: 45, Hercus 2006a), but Kuyani also has *ngutha-ri-* 'get worked up about something,' with the verbal intransitivizing/reciprocal suffix *-ri*, which is clearly reflected in the Barngarla sentence.

7.5.9 Associative *-lyga, -lyganha*

Commonly in Australia possession is indicated by a suffix attached to a noun denoting the thing possessed, and this is what we find in Barngarla.[13] Schürmann spells the Barngarla suffix used for this purpose *ilka* and *ilkanna*, and it is likely that the phonemic shape of this form was *-lyga* and *-lyganha*. This is the ASSOCIATIVE suffix, and indicates that something is closely associated with (such as being in the possession of) something or someone else. An example of this use is seen here:

(7.26)	kaya-ilka	padnatanna
(=12.8a)	gayalyga	badnadhanha
(g14)	gaya-lyga	badna-dha-nha
	spear-ASSOC	go-PRES-2,3.pl

they have spears

Other uses of this suffix do not mark possession specifically, but serve to denote close association, or characterization more generally:

---

[13] *Contra* Hercus (1999: 56).

(7.27a) karkuru ilkanna kauo wornitao
(15) garrgurrulyganha gawu warnidhawu
garrgurru-lyganha gawu warni-dha-wu
whizz-ASSOC water fall-PRES-3.sg.NOM

the rain comes rushing down

(7.27b) Ngaityidnilka ngukat'urro
(43) ngadyidnilyga ngugadhurru
ngadyidni-lyga nguga-dha-urru
1.sg.STEM.2-ASSOC go-pres-2.sg.PATR

On my account or with me dost thou go

I have presumed that the word *karkuru* is onomatapoeic, with trills: *garrgurru*.

Using the words *kaya* 'spear,' *kaka* 'head,' *karkuru* 'whizzing or rustling noise,' *manka* 'cicatrice,' *mayi* 'vegetable food,' *marralyi** 'dry,' and the stem-2 shape of the 1st singular pronoun, phonemic *ngadyidni*, Schürmann records the following inflections. First, with the associative morpheme as an orthographic post-position: *kaya ilka* 'with spears, armed,' *kaka ilka* 'obstinate,' *karkuru ilkanna* 'with a rushing sound;' then hyphenated: *mai-ilkanna* 'having food,' *kaya-ilka* 'with spears;' and then suffixed: *mankailkanna* 'with cicatrices, *kayailka* with spears, armed,' *kutta marralyilkanna* 'no dry-possessing,' and *ngaityidnilka* 'on my account or with me.'

Given the unlikelihood of phonemic diphthongs in Barngarla as discussed in Section 2.4; given Schürmann's orthographic vacillation in these words *(kaya ilka/kaya-ilka/kayailka* in particular); and given his use of the letter *i* to signal raised vowels before lamino-palatal consonants, an analysis describing the lateral *ly* rather than the vowel *i* at the start of this suffix would be consistent with his recorded material.

7.5.10 Privative -*marraba*, -*waga*

Schürmann has two privative suffixes meaning 'not having (something), without (something),' which he spells *wakka* and *marrapa*. Adnyamathanha has privative -*waka* and -*wakanha* (McEntee & McKenzie 1992: 80 in compound *mara-waka* 'without end;' Tunstill 2004: 429), and Kuyani has -*wakanha* (Hercus 2006a). For the other shape, Kuyani has privative -*warrampa*, which Hercus (2006a) compares to the Barngarla form which she spells *marrba*, presumably following the pronunciation of an Adnyamathanha or Kuyani speaker. Schürmann offers the following examples:

(7.28a)　ngai　　palta-marraba
(28)　　 ngayi　 baldhamarraba
　　　　 ngayi　 baldha-marraba
　　　　 I.NOM　 cloak-PRIV
　　　　 I have no cloak

(7.28b)　mena wakka
(31)　　 minawaga
　　　　 mina-waga
　　　　 eye-PRIV
　　　　 honest, not thievish

(7.28c)　kakka wakka
(65)　　 gagawaga
　　　　 gaga-waga
　　　　 head-PRIV
　　　　 headless, stupid

(7.28d) kuya wakka

(65) guyawaga

   guya-waga

   fish-PRIV

   having no fish, or being no fisherman

Schürmann has *mena*, both 'eye' and 'theft,' a word that expresses the idea of hiding in a variety of ways.' 'Eye' is *mina* in both Adnyamathanha (McEntee & McKenzie 1992: 84) and Kuyani (Hercus 2006a). As Schürmann spells both these words the same way, I will assume they are homophones at least, but more likely polysemous, with a common association having to do with visibility or the avoidance of visibility: that is, with concealment.

Eight: Other suffixes

Suffixes are used in Barngarla for many purposes, not just for coding relationships between nouns and other parts of a sentence. The following suffixes may be attached to other parts of speech, as Schürmann notes, and are found 'generally with the last word in a sentence.'

8.1 Grammatical endings

The suffixes in the following list code grammatical meanings that may involve nouns, or which may involve other parts of speech as well, such as (nominalized) verbs, although Schürmann gives only one example of this.

8.1.1 Goal *-lbu*

In his grammar section Schürmann shows this ending used on nouns that are the objects of the verb *kanata* 'wait for,' which he spells *kannata* in his vocabulary. I have been able to find correspondences for neither this verb nor for the suffix he spells *-lbo* in other Thura-Yura languages. The examples he gives are:

(8.1a)   maiilbo   kanaturru

(g8)   mayilbu   ganadhuru

         mayi-lbu   gana-dhu-(a)ru

         food-GOAL   await-PRES-3.sg.ERG

         he waits for food

(8.1b)	paltalbo	kanatarru
(g8)	baldhalbu	ganadharu
	baldha-lbu	gana-dha-aru
	cloak- GOAL	await-PRES-3.sg.ERG

he expects clothing

In the first example, but not the second, it looks like the vowel of the present-tense suffix *-dhu* has harmonized with that of the following 3rd singular ergative suffix *-(a)ru*.

8.1.2 Comparative *-lV*

Adnyamathanha and Kuyani have a comparative suffix *-li* (Tunstill 2004: 428, Schebeck 1974: 8, Hercus 2006c), and Kaurna has *-rli* in this function (Amery & Simpson 2013: 123). I will assume that the Barngarla lateral in this suffix is alveolar like its northern counterparts: again the vowel in this suffix harmonizes with a preceding vowel. Schürmann offers the following:

(8.2a)	yuralla	pony	yerbatunno
(g8)	yurhala	pony	yarrbadhurnu
	yurha-la	pony	yarrba-dh(a)-urnu
	man-LIKE	pony	talk-PRES-2.sg.ERG

like a man you command the pony, ie, you speak to him as if he were a man, able to understand you

(8.2b)	nurkullu	pony	padnatao
(g8)	nhurrgulu	pony	badnadhawu
	nhurrgu-lu	pony	badna-dha-wu
	2.sg.POSS-LIKE	pony	go-PRES-3.sg.NOM

a pony like yours is here

(8.2c)	malbullu	pappi	ngaitye	ikkatao	nurreri
(g8)	malbulu	babi	ngadyi	igadhawu	nhurriri
	malbu-lu	babi	ngadyi	iga-dha-wu	nhurriri
	murderer-LIKE	father	my	sit-PRES-3.sg.NOM	far

my father lives far away like a murderer

Sentence (8.2a) above shows a transitive verb root *yerba- (yarrba- ?)* 'address, command,' not found in Schürmann's vocabulary. Sentence (8.2b) shows a verb *badna-* 'go,' found also in Kaurna as *padni-* (Amery & Simpson 2013: 123). Notice how in this context *badna-* serves an existential meaning, like English *be*. The verb *badna-* is one of a set of Barngarla verbs that serve existential functions (see Section 12.3). The sentence in (8.2c) occurs without a translation, so I have provided one that I hope reflects the speaker's meaning. Schürmann has *nurreri* 'far away,' and *malbu* 'murderer.' The Western Desert dialect Manyjilyjarra has *malpu* 'devil' (Marsh 1992: 38), which may be related to the Barngarla word.

In the sentences above we see the comparative suffix *-IV* attached to nouns and a pronoun. The following sentence shows this suffix attached to a verb. Unfortunately we can only guess at the verb's morphology; here are two options:

(8.3a) (g8)

warru	yantyinilli	yarraityalla	ngammatinni
waru	yandyinili	yarradyala	ngamadhini
waru	yandyi-ni-li	yarradyala	ngama-dha-ini
kangaroo	?hunt-PAST-LIKE	quick	go-PRES-2.sg.NOM

you run so fast as if hunting a kangaroo

(8.3b) (g8)

warru yantyinilli	yarraityalla	ngammatinni
waruyandyinili	yarradyarla	ngamadhini
waru-ya-ndya-ini-li	yarradyarla	ngama-dha-ini
kangaroo-?chase-PERF-2.sg.NOM-LIKE	quick	go-PRES-2.sg.NOM

you run so fast as if hunting a kangaroo

A verb *yantyi-** (option 1 in (8.3a) above) does not appear in another Thura-Yura source, not even in Schürmann's own Barngarla dictionary. However if we could posit such a verb with a meaning 'hunt,' the sentence we see could show this verb with a past-tense suffix plus the comparative suffix. Alternatively, Kuyani has a (possibly reduplicated) transitive verb *yaya-* 'chase, run after' with exactly the semantics required here (Hercus 2006b). If we could posit an intransitive compound *waru-ya-* 'chase kangaroos/kangaroo-chasing' with the stative (perfect aspect, inherently non-agentive) suffix *-ndya*, it could take nominative pronominal suffixes such as that suggested here in option 2 (8.3b). The advantage of this admittedly more complicated option is that it might get around Schürmann's otherwise curious omission from his dictionary of such an important and presumably high-frequency verb as our putative *yandyi-** 'hunt,' as well as avoiding an illegal monosyllabic verb root *ya-*. Schürmann does, however, have *yarraityalla* 'quick;' and Kuyani has *ngama-* 'go along, travel.'

Schürmann describes a truly comparative sense meaning for this suffix when used on adjectives, as *more ___*. He offers just two examples:

| garrala | *higher* | from | garra | *high* | (g9) |
| barhili | *deeper* | from | barhi | *deep, creek* | |

Schürmann has *parri* 'deep, below; river;' this is Kuyani *parhi* (Hercus 2006a) and Adnyamathanha *varhi* (McEntee & McKenzie 1992: 60), both 'creek, river.'

8.1.3 'also' *-indi, -indu*

For this suffix Schürmann offers the following:

(8.4) ngai   Munni indo
(g8)   ngayi   Muniyindu
       ngayi   Muni-y-indu
       1.sg.NOM   name-EP-ALSO

I and Munni, or I (am) also (called) Munni

8.1.4 Manner-adverbial -*gundu*

Of this ending, Schürmann says that it 'corresponds with the English final syllable *ly*.' He offers three examples of its use, the first two using the verb *wangga-* 'speak:'

(8.5a) yalturru   kuntu   wanggakka
(g8)   yaldurrugundu   wanggaga
        yaldurru-gundu   wangga-ga
        bold-MANNER   speak-IMP

speak boldly

(8.5b) Parnkalla   kuntu   wanggakka
(g8)   Barngarlagundu   wanggaga
        Barngarla-gundu   wangga-ga
        LANGUAGE.NAME-MANNER   speak-IMP

speak Parnkalla

For the first sentence the adjective *yalturru* is found in Schürmann's vocabulary as 'bold, fearless, brave.' In the second sentence the name Barngarla is turned into an adverb by means of the suffix -*gundu*, to denote a particular way or manner of speaking, just as 'bold' is turned into an adverb 'boldly,' also to denote a particular way of speaking or behaving.

(8.6a) kaity akkuntu   paru   ngai   nungk'urro
(g8)   gadyagundu   barhu   ngayi   nhunggurru
        gadya-gundu   barhu   ngayi   nhunggu-urru
        child-MANNER   meat   I.NOM   give-2.sg.PATR

very little meat me give thou =
don't give me too much meat / you need only give me a little meat

In sentence example (7.21a) in Section 7.5.5 we saw the word *gadya* used as a noun meaning 'child'. In the sentence above it is turned into an adverb with an apparent meaning 'as (little meat as) you would (give) to a child.' The form of the verb *nhunggu-* 'give' *(nungk'urro)*, however, needs some discussion. This shape is probably hortative, marked by a 2nd singular patrilineal (father and child) short-form pronoun subject *((nh)urru)*, as indicated by Schürmann's use of an apostrophe, suffixed straight onto the verb root. A second, dispreferred, option would see this shape as a haplologically reduced subjunctive:

(8.6b) nungk'urro

nhunggurhurru

nhunggu-rhu-urru

give-SJTV-2.sg.PATR

you (patrilineal) might give

The resulting string *-rhu-urru*, (SUBJUNCTIVE *rhu* + 2nd singular PATRILINEAL *urru*) would then be reduced to *-rru,* as this process is described in Sections 5.8 & 5.9 in relation to subjunctive forms with 3rd singular ergative subjects. Schürmann's translation, however, makes this option unlikely.

8.2 Discourse-pragmatic markers

A number of endings serve to locate what someone is saying within the context of a particular discourse or situation. These suffixes are not used to code grammatical meaning in a strictly formal sense; rather they serve to signal a speaker's attitude, assumptions or stance with respect to some event or some unfolding situation. Some of these endings are listed here.

8.2.1 Interrogative -*nggarli*

This suffix, which Schürmann spells -*ngkalli*, marks questions. I have been unable to find correspondences for this suffix in contemporary or recently-spoken Thura-Yura languages. An example of its use may be seen in sentence example (4.6b) in Section 4.4.6.

8.2.2 Epistemic -*ndi* and -*gu*

These endings affirm or corroborate some opinion; in using them it would seem that a speaker guarantees the truth of his or her statement. Schürmann's first sentence example, using -*ndi*, includes as well what appears to be an an epistemic adverb, *maitya*, glossed 'expressing assurance, indeed:'

(8.7) (g7)

maitya	Kungka	nunko	yunga?	ngaitye	yungandi
madya	Kungga	nhunku	yunga?	ngadyi	yungandi
madya	Kungga	nhunku	yunga	ngadyi	yunga-ndi
EPIST	NAME	your	elder.brother	my	brother-EPIST

is Kungka your brother then? my brother certainly

Kuyani has *yunga* 'elder brother' (Hercus 2006a). Although further examples of their use would be required before we could be certain that these forms signal an epistemic modal meaning, they are at least good candidates for epistemic status. I have been unable to find correspondences for *maitya* 'EPSISTEMIC' in contemporary or recently-spoken Thura-Yura languages. In the following example, using -*gu*, Kuyani has *ngamarna* 'mother's brother' (Hercus 2006b):

(8.8)	Ngulga	ngaitye	ngammana,	ngannako
(g7)	Ngulga	ngadyi	ngamarna,	nganhagu
	Ngulga	ngadyi	ngamarna	nganha-gu
	NAME	my	mother's.brother	who-EPIST

Ngulga is my uncle, what else (should he be)

8.2.3 Satisfaction or joy -*nda*

This suffix Schürmann says expresses satisfaction or joy, probably at finding something you have been looking for, or are pleased with:

(8.9a)   ngaitye   ngammannanda
(g7-8)   ngadyi   ngamarnanda

         ngadyi   ngamarna-nda
         my   mother's.brother-JOY

my uncle!

(8.9b)   palta   ngaityinda
(g8)   baldha   ngadyinda

         baldha   ngadyi-nda
         cloak   my-JOY

my cloak!

8.2.4 Topic -*dyi*

Hercus (2006a) has Kuyani -*tyi* as an emphatic clitic, as does Tunstill for Adnyamathanha (2004: 431). But as Hercus lists no less than ten emphatic suffixes altogether in Kuyani, it is likely that some at least of these code something other than emphasis alone. Schürmann has -*itye*, of which he notes 'the meaning of this suffix which is in frequent use is difficult to describe,' and offers as an example the following:

(8.10)   ngatta   yurringutu   ngattuitye
(g7)   ngadhu   yurhingudhu   ngadhudyi

         ngadhu   yurhi-ngu-dhu   ngadhu-dyi
         1.sg.ERG   understand-APPL-PRES   1.sg.ERG-TOP

I understand well enough

Thura-Yura languages have *yurhi* 'ear' (eg Nhukunu: Hercus 1992: 34, Adnymathanha: McEntee & McKenzie 1992: 104, Wirangu: Miller et al: 2010: 95, Kuyani: Hercus 2006a). Kuyani has a verb *yurhiyagu* 'hear, understand,' and Barngarla has both *yurriti (yurhidhi)* 'hear' and applicative *yurringutu (yurhi-ngu-dhu)* 'understand.'

By one widely-held definition, a topic is something the speaker wants to highlight or bring to the fore in his or her listener's attention. By another, a topic is a grammatical marking that links a referent across a number of consecutive clauses (Dixon 2002: 520). Although we have no extended texts in Barngarla, both these definitions are consistent with the marking of the pronoun in its second occurrence with the suffix *-dyi* in the sentence example above. The frequent use of this suffix on demonstrative pronouns likewise makes it likely that TOPIC is what is being marked here; note forms like *inhadyi* 'this,' *inhadyingi* 'here,' and *bardnidyi* 'this here,' all including the suffix *-dyi*, and one ending in LOCATIVE *-ngi*. For further examples see Chapter Nine.

The final two discourse-attitudinal markers we will look at are only found attached to the ends of verbs.

8.2.5 Doubt -*dlV*

This verbal ending is used to 'signify the doubtfulness of what one says.' The vowel harmonizes with the final vowel of whatever comes in front of it: in the examples below it appears as *-dla, -dli* and *-dlu* respectively. It probably overlaps considerably with the meaning expressed by subjunctive verb forms. Schürmann offers three examples of its use:

(8.11a)   ngukaintyannadla

(g22)   ngugandyanhadla

          nguga-ndya-nha-dla

          go-PERF-2,3.pl-DOUBT

          perhaps they are gone

(8.11b)   ngukaraiidli

(g22)   ngugarhayidli

          nguga-rha-ayi-dli

          go-SJTV-1.sg.NOM-DOUBT

          I may perhaps go

(8.11c) innaityinge   pony   padnatawudlu
(g22)   inhadyingi   pony   badnadhawudlu
         inha-dyi-ngi   pony   badna-dha-wu-dlu
         this-TOP-LOC   pony   go-PRES-3.sg.NOM-DOUBT

it may be that the horse is here

8.2.6 Emphatic-imperative *-lgV*

This ending is suffixed to imperative and hortative verbs to communicate 'intensive meaning,' which seems to indicate that the speaker believes that some action must be performed. Again, the vowel harmonizes with material in front of it. Schürmann lists its vowel-harmonic shapes as *-alka, -ilki,* and *-ulku,* but it is likely that his initial vowels are part of the preceding verb, not the suffix. Schürmann's examples of its use are both in hortative mood:

(8.12a) ngukaiilki
(g22)   ngugayilgi
         nguga-ayi-lgi
         go-1.sg.NOM-EMPH

let me go, or, I will certainly go

(8.12b) kambarrulku
(g22)   gambarulgu
         gamba-aru-lgu
         cook-3.sg.ERG-EMPH

let him cook, ie he shall or must cook

8.3 Derivational/relativizing

Barngarla has a number of ways of forming, or deriving, new words from other, more basic words. We will look at suffixes used with verbs to derive other verbs in Chapter Ten. In this section we will look at two suffixes, *-bidni* and *-rndu*, used to derive adjectives and nouns from other words.

8.3.1 Relativizing *-(b)idni*

As has been seen, a suffix *-dni* or *-rdni* marks ablative meaning on pronouns. This suffix is used as well on nouns, with a somewhat more metaphorical or abstract meaning than that of the ablative suffix *-ngurni* seen in Section 7.5.2. The full shape of the suffix is *-bidni*, with the first sound *b* being dropped 'in most instances,' as Schürmann says. He also states that '*bidni* sometimes stands by itself as a distinct word,' that is, it is not always a suffix; which is what we may be seeing in the sentence examples shown here with the full form *bidni*, instead of its reduced shape. When the short form of this suffix is attached to a noun, it appears that (1) if the noun ends in *a* or *i*, the suffix will be *-idni*, and (2) if the nouns ends in *u*, the suffix will be *-udni*.

Kuyani has a suffix *-pidna* 'ELATIVE, from; out of' (Hercus 2006c), with a meaning that appears to be similar to that of Barngarla *-bidni*. The use of *-bidni* (glossed REL) on nouns is shown in this sentence:

(8.13)	ngadli	kubmanna	ngammibidni
(g6)	ngadli	gubmanha	ngamibidni
	ngadli	[gubmanha	ngami]-bidni
	we.two	[one	mother]-REL

we two are of [from] one mother

Adnyamathanha has *ngami* 'mother' (McEntee & McKenzie 1992: 39), and Kuyani has both *kubma* and *kubmanha* for 'one' (Hercus 2006). In this sentence the phrase *gubmanha ngami* 'one mother' is treated as a unit to which the suffix *-bidni* is attached, as indicated by square brackets. Although an elative meaning (motion out of something) is certainly indicated in this sentence, there is more than simply motion being referred to here: rather the phrase in question denotes parenthood, by metonymical extension. Nevertheless the meanings of derivational/relativizing -*bidni* and ablative -*ngurni* are very close: Schürmann allows both in the following examples:

(8.14a) ngai   warra bidni
(g6)   ngayi   warrabidni
         ngayi   warra-bidni
         1.sg.NOM   far-REL
         I am from far

(8.14b) warra   ngunne
(g6)   warrangurni
         warra-ngurni
         far-ABL
         from far

Evidence for the metaphorical use of -*bidni* is seen in phrases that refer to time: such phrases use passage through space analogically to denote the passage of time:

(8.15a) ngai   yatta bidni
(g9)   ngayi   yadhabidni
         ngayi   yadha-bidni
         I.NOM   now-REL
         I arrived only just now

(8.15b) ngai   paru bidni
(g9)   ngayi   barhubidni
         ngayi   barhu-bidni
         I.NOM   meat/game-REL

I have been hunting

Adnyamathanha has *yatha* 'now' (McEntie & McKenzie 1992: 95).

The metaphorical sense of this suffix is also shown in its power to derive nouns and adjectives from other words. As Schürmann puts it: 'when attached to nouns and other parts of speech [-*bidni*] gives them the power of an adjective.'[14] Here are some more examples of this suffix that Schürmann offers:

(8.16a) karnkurtu bidni yura
(3)   garngurdubidni   yurha
        garngurdu-bidni   yurha
        boat-REL   man

a man of the boat or ship, a sailor

(8.16b) yerkullüdni   yura
(3)   yarrguludni   yurha
        yarrgulu-idni yurha
        before-REL   man

an ancient man, ancestor

(8.16c) nauurri   irrabukarri   guyabidnarri
(7)   Nhawurri   irabugarri   guyabidnarri
        Nhawu-rri   ira-buga-rri   guya-bidna-rri
        NAME-HUM.PL   tooth-rotten-HUM.PL   fish-REL-HUM.PL

the Nauo people have an offensive breath, being fish eaters
Lit: *the Nhawu people have bad teeth, (being) associated with fish*

---

[14] Schürmann 1844, vocabulary section pp 2-3.

(8.16d) wiltyaridni

(3) wildyarhidni

wildyarha-idni

yesterday-REL

of yesterday

(8.16e) kalkarridni

(3) galgarridni

galgarra-idni

long.ago-REL

of old

(8.16f) yatanyarüdni

(3) yadhanyarudni

yadhanyaru-idni

today-REL

of today

In these examples Schürmann has *karnkurtu* 'boat,' clearly based on *garngu* 'house.' Adnyamathanha has *wiltyardla* 'tomorrow' (McKentee & McKenzie 1992: 123), which I will take to be related functionally and formally to Barngarla *wildyarha* 'yesterday,' preserving the retroflexion seen in the Adnyamathanha cluster. Adnyamathanha's *yatha* 'now' reveals the dental consonant in Barngarla *yadhanyaru* 'today.' Kuyani has *kalkathari* (Hercus 2006a) or *kalkatharri* (2006b) 'long ago,' and even *kalkatharipidna* 'from long ago, of old' a calque of the Barngarla word.

The suffix *-bidni* serves a relativizing function, in that it derives adjectval words from other words. Such derived adjectives may then be used to qualify or modify some other word, which now in turn serves as the syntactic head of the expanded phrase. This process can be seen in *garngurdubidni yurha* 'sailor,' where the relativization *garngurdubidni* serves to modify the head noun *yurha*. The same process may be seen in *yarrguludni yurha* 'ancestor' and even in *gubmanha ngamibidni* '(people, unstated) having the same mother.'

Just as the words *gubmanha ngami* 'one mother' are treated as a single expression or phrase which falls in turn under the scope of *-bidni* in the sentence example given in (8.13) above, so do the words *gaya yaburn* 'spear inside' in the following sentence example. The stem *yaburn-* is not listed in Schürmann's vocabulary, but is clearly based on the adverb *yaburhu* 'in, into, within, inside:'

(8.17) (2)

bakukku	kaya	yapurnbidni	paru	ngarrinyuru,	kaitya!
bagugu!	gaya	yaburnbidni,	barhu	ngarinyurhu,	gadya!
bagugu	[gaya	yaburn]-bidni	barhu	ngarinyurhu	gadya
behold	[spear	within]-REL	game	1.du.POSS.PATR	child

behold child! the game is ours, being hit by the spear (Lit: *with a spear inside it*)

The word *bagugu!* 'behold!' looks like an old imperative shape frozen into service as an exclamation.

8.3.2 Intensifying –(aa)rndu

Schürmann refers to another suffix *-nto* or *-ndo*, which he says is used in a similar manner. In Wirangu this is an emphatic suffix *-((g)a)rdu* (Hercus 1999: 28), used to derive, among others, *marnaardu* 'absolutely huge' from *marna* 'big.' Schürmann records the same pair in his grammar, as seen below. On this basis, the phonemic shape of the Barngarla suffix must be *-(aa)rndu*. The suffix seems to be used to derive adjectives from other adjectives or nouns; he offers only three examples:

marnaarndu	*very much*	from	marna	*much, plentiful, large*
badyaarndu	*fierce*	from	badya	*angry*
warlburndu	*hard*	from	warlbu	*bone*
yurrurndu	*very large*	from	?	

Wirangu has *marna* 'a lot, many' and *warlbu* 'bone' (Miller et al 2010: 56, 83); Kuyani has *walpu* 'bone' and *marnarta* 'big' (both Hercus 2006a); and Adnyamathanha has *warlpu* 'bone' (McEntie & McKenzie 1992: 117). The ending *-(aa)rndu* appears to intensify the meaning of the word it is attached to.

Nine: Demonstrative & interrogative pronouns

The northern Thura-Yura languages have a shape *-nha* used as a base for a set of frozen prefixes signalling demonstrative and interrogative meanings:

proximal, *this, here*:	i-	
distal, *that, there*:	ngu-	
interrogative, *who? what?*:	nga-	-nha
interrogative locative, *where? how?*:	wa-	

Schürmann lists two demonstrative pronouns which he spells *inna* 'this,' and *ngunna* 'that,' and two interrogative pronouns *nganna* 'who? what?' and *wanna* which? It seems fairly clear that in these words at least, Schürmann recognized and recorded the apico-dental nasal *nh* as *nn*.

9.1 This & that

Wirangu has *inha* 'this' (Hercus 1999: 64). Kuyani has *nganhanha* 'who?' *ngunha* 'that one over there,' *inha* 'this one,' *wanha* 'where?' and *-matha* 'plural marker' (all Hercus 2006a). Adnyamathanha as well has *inha* 'this,' *ngunha* 'that over there,' *nganha* 'who,' *wanha* 'where' and *-matha* 'plural marker for nouns' with a variant *-mathanha* 'mob, group' (McEntie & McKenzie 1992: 20, 45, 38, 112, 78, Schebeck 1974: 11-13). The singular demonstrative paradigms are as follows:

Schürmann	Phonemic	English
Proximal demonstrative *inha* 'this'		
inna	inha	*this*, NOMINATIVE
innanga	inhanga	*this*, ERGATIVE
innaru	inharhu	*of this*, POSSESSIVE
innardni	inhardni	*from this*, ABLATIVE
innardninge	inhardningi	*with this*, COMITATIVE
innardniru	inhardnirhu	*to this*, ALLATIVE
Distal demonstrative *ngunha* 'that'		
ngunna	ngunha	*that*, NOMINATIVE
ngunnanga	ngunhanga	*that*, ERGATIVE
ngunnaru	ngunharhu	*of that*, POSSESSIVE
ngunnardni	ngunhardni	*from that*, ABLATIVE
ngunnardninge	ngunhardningi	*with that*, COMITATIVE
ngunnardniru	ngunhardnirhu	*to that*, ALLATIVE

All these demonstrative pronouns accept the topic marker *-dyi*, to form pronouns *inhadyi, ngunhadyi* and so on, with the same translations as the forms without topic marking.

These demonstratives may take the dual pronoun marker *-lbili*. Schürmann exemplifies these forms in their nominative case, adding that the rest of the paradigm is 'declined in the same manner as the singular:'

| innalbelli | inhalbili | *these two* |
| ngunnalbelli | ngunhalbili | *those two* |

However when these forms are further inflected, it is not obvious which would come first, the number suffix *-lbili* or the case suffixes.

The human plural marker *-rri* may be added to these demonstratives to make plural shapes: Schürmann offers:

innarri	inharri	*these (people)*
ngunnarri	ngunharri	*those (people)*

But he says it is more usual to add the pluralizing suffix *matta (-madha* 'group'). With this word or suffix at least, we can see that the case inflections come *after* the number-marking suffix:

inna matta	inhamadha	*this mob,* NOMINATIVE
inna mattanga	inhamadhanga	*this mob,* ERGATIVE
inna mattaru	inhamadharhu	*of this mob,* POSSESSIVE … etc
ngunna matta	ngunhamadha	*that mob,* NOMINATIVE
ngunna mattanga	ngunhamadhanga	*that mob,* ERGATIVE
ngunna mattaru	ngunhamadharhu	*of that mob,* POSSESSIVE … etc[15]

9.2   Here & there

Schürmann recorded some DEMONSTRATIVE ADVERBS in Barngarla, as follows:

innaityinge	inhadyingi	*here*
pardni	bardni	*hither, this way*
pardnitye	bardnidyi	*this here*
pardnityinge	bardnidyingi	*here*

---

[15] Note in this 1844 publication an early use of the Aboriginal-English group noun *mob*, applied to people.

patha	badha	*there*
pathara	bathara	*there*
patharu	badharhu	*thither*

These words are formed from base forms *inha* 'this,' *bardni* 'hither' and *badha* 'there,' with the addition of the topic-marking suffix *-dyi*, allative *-rhu*, and the locative suffix *-ngV*. We could expect that forms without topic-marking would also be legal, such as *inhanga* 'here,' and *bardningi* 'hither, towards me.'

9.3 Who? What?

The interrogative pronoun *nganha* refers to both people and things (as both *who?* and *what?*). In Adnyamathanha this word has as well an indefinite meaning, as 'someone' (Schebeck 1974: 13), and it is likely to have had this meaning in Barngarla as well. Despite the Kaurna possessive form *ngangku* 'whose?' (Amery & Simpson 2013: 141), the Barngarla possessive shape that Schürmann spelled *ngankuru* 'whose?' is likely to be phonemic *nganhkurhu*, for reasons canvassed in Section 3.1.7, with regard to the shape of the 2nd singular pronoun. The formations of the interrogative pronoun are as follows:

Interrogative *nganha* 'who? what?'

nganna	nganha	*who, what,* NOMINATIVE
ngannunga	nganhunga	*who,* ERGATIVE
ngankuru	nganhkurhu	*whose,* POSSESSIVE
ngankurni	nganhkurni	*from whom,* ABLATIVE
ngankurninge	nganhkurningi	*with whom,* COMITATIVE
ngankurniru	nganhkurnirhu	*to whom,* ALLATIVE
ngannanga	nganhanga	*in what, wherein,* LOCATIVE
ngannaru	nganharhu	*what for?* PURPOSIVE

Other nominal suffixes can be attached to *nganha;* we have already seen the shape *nganharhu* |nganha-rhu| [what-PURP] 'what for? why?' in sentence example

(7.18b) in Section 7.5.4. Schürmann records another interrogative pronoun with the same meaning as *nganha*: this is *nhaawi* 'what? who?'; as well as its purposive form *nhaawindi* 'what for? why?' With reference to comparable words in the Western Desert Language, it is likely that this pronoun had a long first vowel.

Notice how the language is able to distinguish between uses of at least two multi-functional suffixes: the second vowel of the ergative shape *nganhunga* shows a change from *a* to *u*; while the locative (place where at) shape retains its original second vowel: *nganhanga*. As well, the possessive/allative/purposive suffix *-rhu* is found on both *nganhkurhu* 'whose?' and *nganharhu* 'what for?;' these shapes use different stems to encode their different meanings.

The dual and plural numbers of this pronoun are marked by *-lbili* and *-dhanha* respectively: this latter shape is probably a truncation of the plural marker found in Adnyamathanha as *-mathanha*:

ngannalbelli	nganhalbili	*which two?* DUAL
ngannatanna	nganhadhanha	*which ones?* PLURAL

9.4 Which? Where? How?

The word *wanna* which Schürmann in his grammar translates as 'which,' is *wanha* 'where?' in Adnyamathanha and Kuyani, and includes this meaning in Barngarla as well, as we can see from Schürmann's dictionary on pages 67-68. The southern Thura-Yura languages Kaurna and Nhukunu combine the meanings *where?* and *which?* or *how?* as two senses of the one word: in Kaurna this word is *waatha* 'where?' 'which?' (Amery & Simpson 2013: 147) and in Nhukunu it is *wanhanga* 'where?' 'how?' (with locative inflection) (Hercus 1992: 30). The Barngarla words *wanha* and *waadha* (see below) could mean *which?* or *where?* according to context. Schürmann claims that only one case ending was available to *wanha*, locative *-nga*. However it is likely that other directional affixes would have been used as well, such as *wanharhu?* 'where to?' *waadhanga* 'where at?' and *wanhangurni?* 'where from?' We can assume this because of two other forms meaning 'where?' listed by Schürmann in his vocabulary on page 70, which are the same as the

Kaurna word noted above: *watha* (phonemic *waadha*) 'where?' and *watharu* (phonemic *waadharhu*) 'whither?' Attested and likely forms used for these meanings are shown here:

wanha, waadha	*which? where?*
wanhanga, waadhanga	*wherein? where at?* LOCATIVE
wanharhu, waadharhu	*whither? where to?* ALLATIVE
wanhangurni, waadhangurni	*where from? whence?* ABLATIVE

The use of *waadha* in Barngarla may be seen in sentence example (12.11) in Section 12.4.

A variant of *wanha* is *wandyi* 'how?:' note the sentence:

(9.1) nunko   wantye   metye
(68)   nhunku   wandyi   midyi
       your   how   name

how is your name? [=what is your name?]

Ten: Verbal derivational affixes

Verbal derivational affixes are suffixes or prefixes that turn words into verbs. For example, in English the shape *en* turns adjectives into verbs, such as when the adjective *large* has *en-* put in front of it to make the verb *enlarge* 'cause (something) to become large;' or when the adjective *bright* has *-en* put after it to make *brighten* 'cause (something) to become bright.' So in Barngarla, there are a number of endings that can be used to turn words into verbs, and which can also be used to turn verbs into other verbs. A verb root to which a derivational affix has been added will be referred to as a verb STEM.

10.1 Continuous derivation

Barngarla verbs may take endings that Schürmann spells *-ntutu* and *-nturrutu*, and which are probably phonemic *-ndhudhu* and *-ndhurudhu*. These endings are made up of continuous shapes *-ndhu-* and *-ndhuru-*, plus a present-tense suffix *-dhu*. The shape *-ndhu-* is found on verbs with roots ending in *a* or *i*, and the shape *-ndhuru-* is found on verbs with roots ending in *u*. These endings show us that the action of the verb is going on over some period of time. As we saw in Section 4.2.1, Kuyani has a present-tense suffix *-ntya*, Kaurna has *-nthi* and Adnyamathanha has *-ntha;* it is therefore likely that the shape Barngarla uses to make an ending signalling continuous aspect is *-ndhu*. Here are some examples that Schürmann offers:

Roots ending in *a*:

ngamadha *go, come*	ngamandhudhu *keep going, running*
badnadha *go*	badnandhudhu *keep walking about*
yagadha *seek, look for*	yagandhudhu *(keep) looking for*
igadha *sit, dwell, live*	igandhudhu *remain, stay*
madadha *pick up*	madandhudhu *gather*

Roots ending in *i*:

warnidhi *lie down*	warnindhudhu *remain in a lying posture*

Roots ending in *u*:

mankudhu *take, get*	mankundhurudhu *keep on taking*
nhunggudhu *give*	nhunggundhurudhu *keep on giving*
nhagudhu *see*	nhagundhurudhu *keep on looking*
warrudhu *throw about*	warrundhurudhu *keep on throwing about*

There is a verb *yanturrutu* 'catch,' but this probably contains a stem *yandu-ru-*, and so is not a derived continuous form; it may be reflexive or medio-passive (see Sections 10.4 & 10.5 below).

The shape *-dhu* at the end of these suffixes is a normal present-tense ending, with a vowel *(u)* that harmonizes with the vowel(s) in the shape *-ndhu(ru)-* that comes in front of it. The verbs Schürmann presents in his vocabulary are present-tense continuous forms, and their construction is therefore as follows, for verbs with roots ending in *a*, *i* and *u* respectively:

igandhudhu	warnindhudhu	nhunggundhurudhu
iga-ndhu-dhu	warni-ndhu-dhu	nhunggu-ndhuru-dhu
sit-CONT-PRES	lie-CONT-PRES	give-CONT-PRES
remaining	*keep on lying down*	*keep on giving*

The continuous shape *-ndhu(ru)-* can be used with other tense suffixes, and not just the present-tense one. Schürmann shows us an example with an imperative suffix, but without a gloss; I have provided the translation shown here:

(10.1) mai   nungkunturrukka
(40)   mayi   nhunggundhuruga!
        mayi   nhunggu-ndhuru-ga
        food   give-CONT-IMP

keep on giving food!

Here is another with a past-tense ending, producing a past continuous meaning:

(10.2) patharutye   wannintunn'ai
(g22)   badharhudyi   warnindhunayi
        badharhu-dyi   warni-ndhu-na-ayi
        thither-TOP   lie-CONT-PAST-1.sg.NOM

there I remained lying

Schürmann's vocabulary has *patha* and *pathar*, both 'there,' *patharu* 'thither,' and *patharütye* 'thereabout' (see Section 9.2). This last could be *badha* plus the allative suffix *-rhu* to make an adverb *badharhu* 'thither, over there,' plus the topic marker *-dyi*.

We could also expect to find verb forms like the following:

(10.3) badnandhunu   warnindhurhu
        badna-ndhu-nu   warni-ndhu-rhu
        go-CONT-PAST   lie/fall-CONT-SJTV
        kept walking about   *might keep falling*

        yagandhundya   yagandhuga
        yaga-ndhu-ndya   yaga-ndhu-ga
        seek-CONT-PERF   seek-CONT-IMP
        has/have been searching   *keep on searching!*

Remember that the past tense suffix *-nV* and the subjunctive mood suffix *-rhV* harmonize with vowels that come in front of them. The imperative suffix *-ga* does not appear to harmonize with a preceeding *u*, only with a preceeding *i*.

10.1.1   *-ndhu-* & *-ndhuru-*

A note has been added to Schürmann's grammar to the effect that the affix *-ndhuru* carries middle-voice or reciprocal-continuous meaning, in that it incorporates the intransitive verbalizer *-ri* (see Section 10.2.2 below), which shows up in this environment as *-ru: -ndhu-ru*. This would be logical and consistent, were it not that the forms *-ndhu* and *-ndhuru* are in phonological complementary distribution, as noted. Schürmann appears to draw an analogy between the continuous form *nhunggundhurudhu (nungkunturrutu)* and reciprocal *widiridhi (wittirriti)*. However the reciprocal form of the verb *nhunggu-* 'give' that corresponds to reciprocal *widiridhi* 'spear each other', is both *nhunggungaridhi (nungkungarriti)* 'give to each other, exchange' and *nhungguridhi (nungkurriti)* (see Sections 10.4.2 & 10.4.3 below). Although Schürmann's analysis is appealing on morphological grounds, without further evidence I would be inclined to reject it on phonological grounds.

10.1.2   Reduplication

An event's continuous aspect, or its repetition, its intense occurrence or energetic performance, may all be signalled by reduplication; that is, the doubling-up of a verb root. There are a number of examples of this in Schürmann's vocabulary; for example the root *bada-* 'drive away' may be reduplicated and made intransitive to depict ongoing or multiple acts of driving away: *bada-bada-ri-* 'disperse, scatter.' An example of the use of this verb is shown here:

(10.4)	nungurru	kundatanna	mai	mundulturringe
(40)	nhungurru	gurndadhanha	mayi	munduldurringi,
	nhungurru	gurnda-dha-nha	mayi	munduldu-rri-ngi
	careful	hit-PRES-2,3.pl	food	European-HUM.PL-ERG

kutta	batta battarrini
guda	badabadarini
guda	bada-bada-ri-ni
NEG	dispel-dispel-VBLZR-PAST

the Europeans beat out the food (wheat) carefully, not spilling any

The noun *ngubi* 'darkness' may be reduplicated and made into a verb *ngubu-rubu-ri-* meaning 'be pitch black.' This verb's reduplicated stem is probably constructed as follows: |ngubi$_1$-ri-ubi$_2$-ri| → [dark$_1$-VBLZR-dark$_2$-VBLZR], with the second occurrence of *ngubi (ubi$_2$)* missing its first consonant, and with vowel harmony extending rightwards from the vowel in the first syllable *ngu*. The use of intransitive verbalizers in Barngarla is discused in Section 10.2 below, and in following sections.

And some words are reduplicated simply because they denote messy or scattered things, such as *birrgi-birrgi* 'bit and pieces.'

10.2 Intransitive verbalizers with stative meaning

As pointed out in Section 4.1.2, the distinction between transitive and intransitive verbs is important in Barngarla, although it is not so obviously important in English. Barngarla has one set of derivational suffixes that make intransitive verbs, and another to make transitive verbs. In this section we will look at the endings that make intransitive verbs in Barngarla.

Schürmann records endings he spells *iti* and *nniti*, by means of which 'adjectives … are rendered into verbs.' The last syllable of these shapes is the present-tense suffix *-dhi*. This leaves two endings dedicated to the purpose he states, *-i* and *-ni*. This second shape occurs in his vocabulary spelled *nniti*, *rniti* and once as *rnniti;* the ending appears to be phonemic *-ni* or *-rni*, and it may be that different words select one or the other of these shapes. There is another intransitive verbalizing suffix *-ri,* which he does not mention, but is nonetheless evident in his vocabulary.

Adnyamathanha has intransitive derivational affixes *-i* and *-ri* (Schebeck 1974: 16-18), and Kuyani has intransitive verbalizers *-ni* (Hercus 2006a) and *-ri* (Hercus

2006c). Wirangu has an intransitive verbalizer *-ri*, with stative and inchoative functions (Hercus 1999: 101-102). There is good evidence that Barngarla uses all three of these shapes for this purpose.

10.2.1   Verbalizer *-(r)ni*

When an adjective, a noun or another verb is inflected with one of these suffixes, one or other or two meanings may be signalled. The first meaning is STATIVE: this means that something exists as or in a certain state of being. The following examples show the suffix *-(r)ni* used for this purpose. The first set we will look at are adjectives that are turned into intransitive verbs:

Adjective:	garnba *empty, hungry*	irri *clean*
Intr verb:	garnbanidhi	irrinidhi
	garnba-ni-dhi	irri-ni-dhi
	hungry-VBLZR-PRES	clean-VBLZR-PRES
	being empty, hungry	*being clean*

Adjective:	gangi *self-willed, impetuous, resolute*
Intr verb:	ganginidhi
	gangi-ni-dhi
	resolute-VBLZR-PRES
	being self-willed, resolute

Nouns can also be made into intransitive verbs this way:

Noun:	gaga *head*	gugarha *staff, stick*
Intr verb:	gaganidhi	gugarnidhi
	gaga-ni-dhi	guga-rni-dhi
	head-VBLZR-PRES	staff-VBLZR-PRES
	rising, coming up, growing	*leaning on (something)*

Noun: marrga *one day/24 hours*

Intr verb: marrganidhi

             marrga-ni-dhi

             day-VBLZR-PRES

             staying for a day, staying overnight

Wirangu has *gugura* 'long-handled toy throwing stick' (Miller et al 2010: 40), with a note that this word is widespread around Lake Eyre; Adnyamathanha on the other hand has *kukurha* 'pointed throwing stick used in games' (McEntee & McKenzie 1992: 34). I will prefer McEntee & McKenzie's transcription here, as likely being more reliable in this instance.

In Schürmann's vocabulary there are two transitive verbs that can be made intransitive with this suffix:

Trans verb:	garladha *call, hail (someone)*	guladha *sever, cut, break, tear*
Intrans verb:	garlanidhi	gulanidhi
	garla-ni-dhi	gula-ni-dhi
	call-VBLZR-PRES	tear-VBLZR-PRES
	call out	*be rent, cut, torn*

Kuyani has a transitive verb *karlda-* 'call out to someone' (Hercus 2006a), showing that the lateral cluster here is retroflex.

10.2.2 Verbalizer *-ri*

Although the suffix *-(r)ni* appears to be used more with adjectives and nouns, and with only two verbs, the suffix *-ri* is found on lots of transitive verbs, making them intransitive. Here are some examples from Schürmann's vocabulary:

Trans verb:	badadha *drive, scare away*	ngaradha *conceive, bring out*
Intr verb:	badabadaridhi	ngararidhi
	bada-bada-ri-dhi	ngara-ri-dhi
	dispel-dispel-VBLZR-PRES	produce-VBLZR-PRES

	dispersing	*increasing, multiplying*

Trans verb: yaridhi *put on, cover oneself*

Intr verb: yariridhi

               yari-ri-dhi

               cover-VBLZR-PRES

               being covered

Wirangu has *badabadarn* 'brush off' (Miller et al: 2010: 2), and Adnyamathanha has *ngara-* 'be born, give birth,' and *yari-* 'dress, wear clothes' (McEntee & McKenzie 1992: 40, 98). Barngarla has an idiomatic expression using the derived intransitive verb *yari-ri-* 'be covered:'

(10.5)   penyinge   yarrirriti

(82)   binyingi   yariridhi

           binyi-ngi   yari-ri-dhi

           pain-INST   cover-VBLZR-PRES

           being covered with pain, feel pain all over the body

The suffix *-ri* is also used on *in*transitive verbs to produce *other* intransitive verbs: it is not always evident how these newly derived verbs are different in meaning from their original underived versions; only access to the way language was used by native speakers with full control of their language would allow us to discover some of the differences in meaning here. Some examples Schürmann has in his vocabulary are the following:

Intr verb: galgudhu *be in pain*   malidhi *slip, fall*

Derived intr verb: galguridhi   maliridhi

                       galgu-ri-dhi   mali-ri-dhi

                       pain-VBLZR-PRES   slip-VBLZR-PRES

                       being sick   *dissolving, being powerless*

Intr verb:	iridhi *move, shift*	warnadha *abound, be plentiful*
Derived intr verb:	iriridhi	warnaridhi
	iri-ri-dhi	warna-ri-dhi
	move-VBLZR-PRES	abound-VBLZR-PRES
	keep moving, be restless	*abound, be confused*

Intr verb:	marrgadha *be stuck, be tight*	binyidhi *be painful, hurt*
Derived intr verb:	marrgaridhi	binyiridhi
	marrga-ri-dhi [16]	binyi-ri-dhi
	stick-VBLZR-PRES	pain-VBLZR-PRES
	adhering, sticking	*feeling pain*

Adjectives as well may take the suffix *-ri* to form intransitive verbs:

Adjective:	ganu-ganu *sheltered, warm*	mawurhu *black*
Intr verb:	ganu-ganuridhi	mawurhuridhi
	ganu-ganu-ri-dhi	mawurhu-ri-dhi
	warm-REDUP-VBLZR-PRES	black-VBLZR-PRES
	feeling hot	*being black*

Adjective:	mandha *moist, wet*
Intr verb:	mandharidhi
	mandha-ri-dhi
	moist-VBLZR-PRES
	be moist, wet

Wirangu has *marhu* 'black' (Miller et al 2010: 57), Kuyani has *mantha-mantha* 'moist, fresh' (Hercus 2006a), and Adnyamathanha has *mantha* 'fresh (as meat).'

---

[16] This root is probably homophonous with *marrga* 'day' seen in Section 10.2.1 above.

Just as only two transitive verbs in Schürmann's vocabulary take the intransitive verbalizing suffix -(r)ni, so only two nouns take the verbalizer -ri:

Noun:	binyi *pain, hurt*	wirrubu *row, line*
Intr verb:	binyiridhi	wirrubaridhi
	binyi-ri-dhi	wirruba-ri-dhi
	pain-VBLZR-PRES	line-VBLZR-PRES
	feeling pain	*forming a line*

A number of adjectives end in the sounds -ra, -rhu or -ru. When the intransitive verbalizer -ri is attached to these adjectives, the -ra, -rhu or -ru sound is usually (but not always) dropped off. This means that sequences that may have started out as -ra-ri, -rhu-ri and -ru-ri all end up as -ri. Some of these adjectives and their corresponding intransitive verbs are shown here:

Adjective	Derived intransitive verb
yanga<u>ra</u> *broad, wide*	yangaridhi *extending, spreading*
warlbu<u>ru</u> *strong, headstrong*	warlburidhi *being strong, being persistent*
wirlu<u>rhu</u> *long, tall*	wirluridhi *being long, being tall*
wanyba<u>ra</u> *sad*	wanybaridhi *feeling sad and lonely*
bila<u>ra</u> *sparse*	bilaridhi *being sparse*
mana<u>ra</u> *slow, lazy*	manaridhi *being slow, lazy*
barlba<u>ra</u> *dusty*	barlbaridhi *feel itchy, uncomfortable*

Adnyamathanha has *mana-mana* 'very slow, lazy' (McEntee & McKenzie 1992: 78), and *warlburu* 'strong' is from *warlbu* 'bone.'

10.2.3 Verbalizer *-i*

The third intransitive verbalizer that Barngarla uses is *-i*: this shape replaces the final vowel of words that end in *a* and *i*. When a word root ends in *u*, the verbalizer *-i* changes to *-u* in harmony with that vowel. Here are some examples in three sets: the first set contains roots ending in *a*, the second roots ending in *i*, and the third contains roots ending in *u*:

Roots ending in *a*:

Barngarla	*language name*	barngarlidhi	*speak Barngarla*
bagamba	*full*	bagambidhi	*be full*
bumbara	*plentiful, abundant*	bumbaridhi	*be plentiful, abound*
ildarla	*choked*	ildarlidhi	*be choked, breath heavily*

Roots ending in *i*:

binyi	*pain*	binyidhi	*be painful, hurt*
gabmidi	*wise, knowing*	gabmididhi	*become wise, learn*
yurhi mandyarri	*glad, merry*	yurhi mandyarridhi	*be pleased*

Roots ending in *u*:

gumbu	*urine*	gumbudhu	*wet with urine*
yalygu	*together, in company*	yalygudhu	*put together (come together?)*
marnaarndu	*very much*	marnaarndudhu	*become large, grow*
Munduldu	*European*	munduldidhi	*live in a European manner*

Of course with pairs like *manara* 'slow' and *manaridhi* 'be slow,' and *bumbara* 'abundant' and *bumbaridhi* 'abound,' it is impossible to tell whether final *ra* has been dropped and the verbalizer *-ri* added, or if *a* has been replaced by the verbalizer *-i*. But the outcomes are the same either way. The idiom *yurhi mandyarri* 'glad, merry, in good humour' is literally 'ear (=understanding) *(yurhi)* + right *(mandyarri)*.'

10.2.4 Multiple derivations

You may have noticed that some words may be verbalized in more than one way: that is to say, that one root may accept (probably up to) two of the verbalizers *-i, -ri* and *-(r)ni*. Some of these multiple derivations are shown in Table 10.1 at the end of this chapter, in three columns with the translations given by Schürmann; again, it is often impossible to know what differences in meaning these different derivations signalled, or if any difference in meaning at all was signalled.

From the sentence example Schürmann offers in Table 10.1, the core function of the word *munu-munu* 'at once' seems to have been as an expression of impatience; hence the meaning of the verbalization seen here. Adnyamathanha has *varlpa* 'ashes' and *vundhu-thi-* 'blow dust off' (McEntee & McKenzie 1992: 62, 73).

10.3 Inchoative

The second meaning able to be conveyed by these suffixes is INCHOATIVE. This signals that some event, act or performance is beginning, or is becoming, or turning into something else: it depicts a state that has not yet been attained, but one which is on the point of being attained, or which is coming into being. We have already seen four derivations with this meaning, in *gabmidi* 'wise, knowing' → *gabmididhi* 'become wise, learn,' *yuga* 'black' → *yuganidhi* 'become black,' *Munduldu* 'European' → *'munduldidhi* 'become (like) a European,' and *marnaarndu* 'very much' → *marnaarndudhu* 'become large, grow.' This last is based on the adjective *marna* 'much, plentiful, large,' which not only gives the adverb *marnaarndu* 'very much' and the inchoative verb *marnaarndudhu* 'increase, grow,' but also another inchoative verb *marnanidhi* 'become plentiful.'[17] Incidentally, Schürmann's sentence example for this verb shows a derived form inflected for tense and mood endings other than present/future tense:

(10.6) ngai kudlu mannannintyara
(27)   ngayi gudlu marnanindyarha
       ngayi gudlu marna-ni-ndya-rha
       I   louse   many-VBLZR-PERF-SJTV

I may have become full of lice

Kuyani has *kudlu* 'louse' (Hercus 2006a).

---

[17] Expressions denoting quantity, number and size are frequently collapsed; for example the Latin adjective *multus* denotes both a large quantity and a large number, while *parvus* denotes both a small quantity and small size.

The inchoative verbs *gabmididhi*, *munduldidhi* and *marnaarndudhu* all show derivation by means of the *-i/-u* verbalizer. Apart from these, there are few inchoative verbs that are formed this way. A few more are formed using the verbalizer *-ri*:

birrgi-birrgi	*piecemeal, in pieces*	birrgi-birrgi<u>ri</u>dhi	*fall, crumble to pieces*
wagari	*asunder, in pieces, broken*	waga<u>ri</u>dhi	*fall asunder, break*
mangiri	*well, healthy*	mangi<u>ri</u>dhi	*become well, convalesce, heal*
nhani	*harmless*	nhani<u>ri</u>dhi	*become blunt*

And by far the most are formed using the verbalizer *-(r)ni*, which seems to be especially dedicated to signalling inchoative meaning. Important inchoative verbs meaning 'die, go out of existence' are formed from the negative adverbs *madla* and *maga*:

madla	*no, none*	madlanidhi	*become no more, die*
maga	*not so, it is not*	magarnidhi	*be no more, die*
imbanha	*ashes*	imbarnidhi	*become ashy*
ganya	*stone, rock*	ganyanidhi	*become stone, harden, be obstinate*
marna	*many*	marnanidhi	*become plentiful*
mirla	*bad, wicked*	mirlanidhi	*become bad*
mingga	*sore, sick, ill*	minggarnidhi	*become sore, ill*
murla	*dry, dry land*	murlanidhi	*become dry*
badya	*angry*	badyanidhi	*become angry*

Wirangu has *mirla* 'lecherous' (Miller et al 2010: 60) and Adnyamathanha has *murla warru mityi* 'chant for stopping rain' (McEntee & McKenzie 1992: 91) which probably contains *murla* 'dry.' Adnyamathanha also has *imba* 'ash' (McEntee & McKenzie 1992: 21).

10.4 Reflexive & reciprocal verbs

Barngarla has a suffix that Schürmann spells *-ngarri*, that signals both reflexive and reciprocal meanings. Adnyamathanha has a reflexive suffix *-ngkari*, (Schebeck 1974: 19). The Barngarla shape is probably a variant on the Adnyamathanha reflexive suffix, as *-ngari*, because, as Simpson & Hercus point out (2004: 190), a number of sonorant-stop clusters in Adnyamathanha (such as *ngk*) correspond sporadically to simple sonorants (such as *ng*) in Barngarla (see Section 10.8.3 for further discussion). Although reflexive and reciprocal meanings each have their own dedicated suffixes in Adnyamathanha, those meanings share this same suffix in Barngarla.

The Adnyamathanha reciprocal suffix is *-ngurhi* (Schebeck 1974: 19), which it shares with Barngarla, and in Barngarla as well it appears to code primarily reciprocal meaning. The meanings of these suffixes may be summarized as follows:

-ngari	reflexive & reciprocal
-ngurhi	reciprocal

10.4.1 Reflexive & reciprocal meanings

REFLEXIVE meaning in English is often signalled by pronouns ending in *-self*: *myself, herself, themselves*, and so on, where these pronouns serve as objects of transitive verbs. So for the transitive verb *ask*, for example, I can *ask a shopkeeper*, where *shopkeeper* is the object, or I can *ask myself*, where *myself* is the object; and this makes a reflexive expression. However not all reflexive meanings are marked as reflexive. For example, the expression *I'm shaving* has reflexive meaning, but no reflexive marking. In English we just assume that an expression like *I'm shaving* means that I'm shaving myself: to say *I'm shaving myself* sounds kind of odd, except in a hospital setting of some sort. We can, of course, always add a non-reflexive object in an expression such as *I'm shaving my uncle's whiskers*, where *my uncle's whiskers* is the object of *shave*.

Languages differ as to which kinds of action get openly marked as being reflexive, and which don't. In English *I'm shaving* isn't marked as being reflexive, but in French it is: *je me rase* has the pronoun *me* 'myself,' in an expression that translates literally as *I shave myself*. In English the sentence *I'm called Jake* has no reflexive marking and no reflexive meaning; whereas in French it has reflexive marking (the pronoun spelled *m'*), but still no reflexive meaning: *je m'appelle Jacques*; literally *I call myself Jake*, but with the same meaning as English *I'm called Jake*.

In English RECIPROCAL meaning is often marked by the expression *each other*: so, *ask each other, hug each other*, and so on. Reciprocal expressions always involve plural subjects: you can say *they are painting each other*, but never **he is painting each other*. And there is a difference in meaning between reciprocal *they are painting each other* and reflexive *they are painting themselves*. And again, reciprocal meaning is not always marked as such. A verb like *fight* can be used transitively as in *they're fighting the grassfire*, where *grassfire* is the object, or intransitively and reciprocally as in *they're fighting*. An expression like this in English is necessarily understood as being reciprocal: *they're fighting* means that they're fighting each other.

What reflexive and reciprocal constructions have in common, is that the subjects of a reflexive or reciprocal verb are the same people as the verb's objects. So in *I ask myself* the person doing the asking is the same person as he or she who is being asked. And in *they're hugging each other*, the people doing the hugging are the same as those being hugged. While languages like English and Adnyamathanha distinguish between reflexive and reciprocal meanings, many languages, like Barngarla, may not.

10.4.2 Verbalizer *-ri* as reflexive/reciprocal marker

Just as English has expressions like *I'm shaving* and *they're fighting*, where reflexive and reciprocal meanings are not signalled openly, but are present nonetheless, so in Barngarla some verbs may have dervived reflexive or reciprocal meanings without showing the reflexive/reciprocal suffix *-ngari* or the reciprocal suffix *-ngurhi*. Verb forms of this sort that Schürmann offers in his grammar and vocabulary are all derived with the intransitive verbalizer *-ri*:

Reciprocal:

    yabmidhi *scold, abuse*   yabmiridhi *quarrel, abuse each other*

    wididhi *spear*   widiridhi *spear each other*

yalbadha *hate*	yalba<u>ri</u>dhi *hate each other, be enemies*
nhunggudhu *give*	nhungu<u>ri</u>dhi *exchange*

Reflexive:

nhambadha *cover*	nhamba<u>ri</u>dhi *cover oneself, be covered*
budlidhi *turn upside down*	budli<u>ri</u>dhi *turn oneself over*
yalgadha *warm up (by a fire)*	yalgalba<u>ri</u>dhi *make oneself warm*
ngudhadha *loosen, untie*	ngudharidhi *quarrel, argue*

It is not clear what the difference in meaning between *yalgadha* and *yalgalbaridhi* might be, but then language is full of redundancies like this. There is likewise no apparent difference in meaning between the derived intransitive verb *widiridhi* 'spear each other' seen above, and an alternative version *widingaridhi*, without a gloss, but containing the reflexive/reciprocal suffix and which clearly must mean 'spear each other' as well (see Section 10.4.3 below). Note that the root of the verb meaning 'exchange' is *nhungu-*, which is different from the root meaning 'give' upon which it is based, *nhunggu-*. This alternation between the velar nasal *ng* and its post-stopped counterpart *ngk/ngg*, will be noted again in Section 10.8.3. As we shall see, there are other ways as well of deriving a verb meaning 'exchange' from a verb meaning 'give.'

10.4.3 Reflexive/reciprocal *-ngari* & reciprocal *-ngurhi*

Some of the reciprocal and reflexive verbs found in Schürmann's vocabulary with the suffix *-ngari* are listed below, with the transitive verbs from which they are derived:

Reflexive

nhurdudhu *fill, press in*	nhurdungaridhi *rub (oneself)*
buludhu *wipe, brush, sweep*	bulungaridhi *wipe oneself, wash*
yarlidhi *lay hold, detain*	yarlingaridhi *hide oneself*
irradha *keep off, defend, protect*	irrangaridhi *disengage oneself*
	warringaridhi *cut oneself*

Reciprocal

nhalhadha	*name, call*	nhalhangaridhi	*fight*
garadha	*pick a fight (with s'one)*	garangaridhi	*fight (each other)*
garladha	*call, hail*	garlangaridhi	*call to each other*
nhunggudhu	*give*	nhunggungaridhi	*exchange*
wididhi	*spear, pierce*	widingaridhi	*spear each other*

Schürmann has *badya garadha* 'commence a quarrel' as an illustration of the transitive verb *garadha*. *Badya* is an adjective 'angry,' and the relationship here is probably the same as that between *nhalhadha* and *nhalhangaridhi* also seen in the above table.

Some of the semantic connections between transitive verbs and their reflexive/reciprocal counterparts may only have been obvious within some discourse context. Occasionally Schürmann offers such a context, as with the non-obvious connection between *nhurdudhu* 'fill, press in' and *nhurdungaridhi* 'rub (oneself):'

(10.7a) paipa nurtutu
(41)   paipa nhurdudhu
        paipa nhurdu-dhu
        pipe   press-PRES
        to fill the pipe

(10.7b) mena   nurtungarriti
(41)   mina   nhurdungaridhi
        mina   nhurdu-ngari-dhi
        eye   press-RFLX-PRES
        to rub one's eyes

Again, there is little or no point in trying to translate reflexive/reciprocal meanings from one language to another: 'be named' is a formally reflexive verb in French and Barngarla, but not in English (see Section 10.5.2).

The reciprocal suffix *-ngurhi* occurs relatively infrequently in Schürmann's vocabulary; and when it appears, it seems almost invariably to signal reciprocal meaning. Three of the six forms occurring in the vocabulary are shown here:

wanggadha	*speak*	wanggangurhidhi	*converse, talk together*
yarnbadha	*send, dismiss, order*	yarnbangurhidhi	*send to each other*
ira	*tooth*	irangurhidhi	*to gnash the teeth*

As Schürmann does not provide a translation for *yarnbangurhidhi*, I have proposed one here. The verb *irangurhidhi* may be construed as reciprocal in so far as the teeth are grinding against each other.

Two more verbs are found with a shape *-na-* occurring before the reciprocal suffix, to make a morphology *-na-ngurhi*:

budnadha	*come, return*	budna<u>na</u>ngurhidhi	*visit each other*
badya	*anger*	badya<u>na</u>ngurhidhi	*quarrel, fall out*

A comparable phenomenon is described in Section 10.5.2 below, and as in that section, I will propose that the segment -<u>na</u>- seen in these verbs is a vowel-harmonic variant of the derivational morpheme *-ni-* described in Section 10.2.1 above, forming a verb marked with two derivational morphemes. This appears certainly to be the case with the adjective *badya*, verbalized here by means of *-na/ni-*.

10.4.4 Case-marking

As the expressions we have been looking at so far in this chapter have all contained derived intransitive verbs, we may expect them to require nominative-case subjects. However Schürmann offers no sentence examples that clearly show reflexive/reciprocal verbs with stated subjects, so we have no direct evidence as to what case the subjects of such verbs take. In some Australian languages, such as the Western Desert Language, verbs with reflexive/reciprocal marking require ergative case subjects, but Thura-Yura languages appear to be different. In line with the middle-voice meaning of some reflexive/reciprocal-marked Barngarla verbs (see Section 10.5 below), we could expect nominative-case subjects; and this is the situation as well in Wirangu, where reflexive/reciprocal verbs take nominative subjects (Hercus 1999: 109). Schebeck, too, with reference to Adnyamathanha, states that Adnyamathanha verbs with the reflexive suffix *-ngkari* (= Barngarla *-ngari*) are 'always construed intransitively' (Schebeck 1974: 252).

10.5 Middle verbs

Many intransitive verbs bear the stem shape *-ri* in their make-up, without appearing to be derived from any base form to be found in Schürmann's dictionary. These may represent gaps in Schürmann's vocabulary, where he simply has not recorded base forms, or they may represent a class of intransitive verbs that are always uttered with the stem shape *-ri-* appearing after a bi- or even a trisyllabic root. And if this is the case, as it is likely to be, then Barngarla may claim to have a distinct class of MIDDLE verbs, that is, a class of verbs that may not occur without a dedicated intransitivizing morphology built into their composition. Some examples of this class are *mirrgaridhi* 'be startled,' *balgiridhi* 'crack, break, become loose,' *barlagaridhi* 'rise, get up, hasten,' *barlaridhi* 'shine, be lighted, enlightened,' *biyi-biyiridhi* 'blush, be shy, ashamed,' *muwaridhi* 'be engaged in,' and *gudliridhi* 'be silent, sullen.' All of these meanings are entirely consistent with their verbs' middle-voicing morphology.[18]

10.5.1 Conflation of reflexive/reciprocal/middle

Many verbs with reflexive/reciprocal marking in Barngarla also carry MEDIO-PASSIVE or MIDDLE VOICE meaning, in which some activity denoted by a verb involves only the actor, with no other person or thing being concerned. Note that although these verbs bear reflexive/reciprocal morphology *(-ngari,* and in one istance *-ngurhi),* they do not have reflexive/reciprocal meanings. Some of these are listed here:

---

[18] These verbs are analogous to middle verbs in Homeric Greek, such as δύναμαι 'I can,' ἱκνέομαι 'I arrive' and ἀμείβομαι 'I answer.'

Transitive verb	Medio-passive verb
yardadha *cover, shut*	yardayangaridhi *be choked, shut up*
milidhi *do, make*	milingaridhi *busy oneself, work*
marnidhi *smell*	marningaridhi *smell*
nhagudhu *see, understand*	nhagungaridhi *be of dim sight, be about to die*
	ngarragungaridhi *be pretty*
	bidlangaridhi *walk slowly, tarry*
binkyadha *call, name*	binkyangurhidhi *be named*

Note the final verb *binkyangurhidhi* formed with the erstwhile reciprocal suffix *-ngurhi*.

While we cannot be sure of the difference in meaning between *marnidhi* and *marningaridhi*, both meaning 'smell,' we can easily guess: the transitive verb *marnidhi* probably means 'perceive an odour' *(I smell a dead fish)*, while the medio-passive verb *marningaridhi* probably means 'emit an odour' *(that dead fish smells)*. One of the problems encountered in Schürmann's vocabulary may be exemplified by the following observation: he lists verbs *nunata* 'push' and *nunangarriti* 'lie sleeping.' Because we don't know the shape of the second nasal in these verbs *(nh, n,* or *rn)* we cannot tell if the intransitive meaning is derived from the transitive, or if they represent two distinct lexical entries (which seems more likely, going by their translations).

Other verbs with reflexive/reciprocal/middle marking have the same, or almost the same translations as their transitive counterparts: these must represent transitive and intransitive sense meanings, respectively, of the action depicted, as we see with *marnidhi* and *marningaridhi* above. But again, we would have to observe the use of these forms in some discourse context to discover their meanings more precisely. Some that Schürmann lists are shown here:

Transitive verb	Medio-passive verb
nhambidhi *lick*	nhambingaridhi *lick*
nguwadha *ask, entreat, pray*	nguwangaridhi *entreat*

yurrulbudhu *accompany, bring, follow*   yurrulbungaridhi *follow, accompany*

10.5.2   Double derivational marking

Just as the French verb 'to be called/named,' *s'appeller*, has reflexive morphology, so has the equivalent verb in Barngarla, *barlaningaridhi* 'to be named, have the name.' This verb is composed of the following parts:

barla-ni-ngari-dhi

name-VBLZR-RFLX-PRES

is/am/are called ___

This is one of four verbs in Schürmann's vocabulary with a form *-ni-, -i-* or *-ri-* appearing before the reflexive/reciprocal suffix *-ngari*. In Section 10.4.3 we saw a comparable (vowel-harmonic) shape *-na-* inserted before the reciprocal suffix *-ngurhi*, in verbs with reciprocal meanings.

We know that the shape *-ni-* here is an intransitive verbalizing affix because Barngarla verb roots may (usually at least) contain only two syllables. Another verb more clearly shows two versions, one with an intransitive verbalizer, and the other with both an intransitive verbalizer *and* the reflexive/reciprocal suffix; these are based on the noun and adjective *wayi* 'fear, afraid':

Base	Derived with *-ni/i*	Derived with *-ni/i/ri-ngari*
wayi *fear*	wayi<u>ni</u>dhi *be afraid*	wayi<u>ni</u>ngaridhi *be afraid*
mina *eye*		mina<u>ri</u>ngaridhi *deny*
—	barla<u>ni</u>dhi *pronounce, name*	barla<u>ni</u>ngaridhi *be named*
yurhi mandyarri *happy*	yurhi mandyarri<u>i</u>dhi *be happy*	yurhi mandyarri<u>ri</u>ngaridhi *be happy*

Going by their English translations, none of the verbs in the right-hand column have reflexive or reciprocal meanings: rather they describe internal psychological states, or situations that refer only to their subjects. Again, there is no apparent difference in meaning between the two verbs based on *wayi*, nor the two based on *yurhi mandyarri*. The noun *mina* 'eye' is used in a number of predicates having to do with hiding, avoiding and concealing, and the verb *minaringaridhi* clearly shows what must be a verbalizer *-ri* in front of the reflexive/reciprocal suffix. From its translation, the meaning of the verb *barlanidhi* would appear to be transitive, yet it is labelled in Schürmann's vocabulary as *v.* (verb); this is how he usually labelled intransitive verbs. Transitive verbs are labelled *v.a.* (active verb), so we may presume that Schürmann could have understood *barlanidhi* to be intransitive (as its form, with intransitivizing *-ni*, confirms). A better translation of this verb may have been 'recite' or 'declaim.'

10.6 Present participles

A property that appears to be confined to derived intransitive verbs, is the capacity to form present participles (verbal adjectives) by way of a suffix that Schürmann spells as both *-ndi* and *-nti*. Although this ending could be a variation upon the ubiquitous Thura-Yura present-tense shape *-ndhi*, we have no evidence for this one way or the other. The only verbs from which such participles may be formed, are those derived by way of the verbalizing suffix *-ri*. Examples of these participles found in Schürmann's vocabulary, along with the derived verbs from which the participles are in turn derived, are shown below:

Derived intransitive verb	Present participle
gadliridhi *slip, graze*	gadlirindi *slipping, grazing*
gaguridhi *wish, desire, like*	gagurindi *wishing, intending*
gudliridhi *be silent, sullen*	gudlirindi *being silent*
mawurhuridhi *be black*	mawurhurindi *being black*
padlaridhi *play*	padla-padlarindi *playing, joking*
bidniridhi *tarry behind*	bidnirindi *tarrying*
garnmiridhi* *be encircled*	garnmirindi *being encircled*

The final two items in this list are less than completely certain: *bidnirindi* is questioned in Schürmann's vocabulary, and while intransitive *garnmiridhi** 'be encircled, enclosed' is not found there, it may be confidently predicted on the basis of the adjective *garnmi* 'encircled, enclosed,' and causative *garnmiringudhu* 'encircle, enclose, defend, screen' (see Section 10.7.1 below). The word *mawurhurindi* has no gloss in Schürmann's vocabulary; the translation provided here is likely. There is as well an adjective *yuwindi* 'friendless, without relatives,' and a verb *yuwidhi* 'ward off ?:' these words may or may not be related. Schürmann was unsure of the meaning of this verb in any case. For Wirangu Hercus (1999: 119-129) lists a number of verbal participial functions signalled by a number of suffixes, almost any one of which could correspond to the forms under consideration here. Unfortunately Schürmann offers very few sentence examples of these; the most convincing is:

(10.8)   kakkurindinge   wappetanna

(10)   gagurindingi   wabidhanha

         gagu-ri-ndi-ngi   wabi-dha-nha

         intend-VBLZR-PPL-ERG   do-PRES-2,3.pl

         they do it intentionally

Adnyamathanha has *wapi-* 'make up (a song)' (McEntee & McKenzie 1992: 112), and Schürmann has *wabidhi* 'do, make.'

10.7 Causative

As well as having affixes that turn words, including transitive verbs, into *in*transitive verbs, Barngarla also has affixes *-ngu* and *-nggu* that turn intransitive verbs into *transitive* verbs. These suffixes (really variants on a single form) are used as well to enable transitive verbs take on more than one object. Adnyamathanha and Kuyani too have transitive derivational affixes *-ngu* and *-ngku* (Schebeck 1974: 16-18, Hercus 2006a). The form *-ngu* is more common in Barngarla, with *-nggu* being less common. The usual kind of transitive derivation is causativization: that is, turning a transitive predicate into one that expresses cause or causation.

English has causative verbs, the most common being *make*, as applied to an expression such as *he went* to turn it into *I made him go*. Here *made him go* means *caused him to go*. Some verbs have causative meaning built-in: *raise* means *cause (something) to go up*, as in *the flag went up* versus *I raised the flag* (= *I made the flag go up*). Sometimes verbs can be used either intransitively, such as *run* and *sit* in *he ran* and *he sat*, or with causative meaning, as in *I ran them down the chute (= I caused them to run ...)* and *I sat him down (= I caused him to sit down/ I made him sit down).*

While Barngarla does not have distinct causative verbs like English *make*, the affix *-ngu* does very much the same work. Some Barngarla intransitive verbs, and their transitive, causative counterparts are shown in Table 10.2 at the end of this chapter. With reference to this table, Schürmann's dictionary has *mangalla* 'peaceable, friendly,' the base for *mangarlidhi;* and *murriri* 'well, healthy,' the base for *murriridhi*. The dictionary also lists a verb *wanningutu* 'give,' different from the usual verb with this meaning, which is *nhunggudhu*. This may be unrelated to *warnidhi* 'fall,' or it may be a euphemism from the causative derivation *warningudhu* 'drop, let fall,' along the lines, drop (something) → release possession of it → pass possession to someone else. Where Schürmann has *puttutu* 'ache, tear,' Kuyani has an intransitive verb *puthurru-ni-* 'break to pieces,' which Hercus (2006a) also spells *puturru-ni-*, and which may be related to the Barngarla word meaning 'ache.'

For reasons that will become apparent, the causative morpheme will be glossed APPL (applicative) in sentence examples. Schürmann offers very few sentences to illustrate causative constructions, but one example he does show is the following:

(10.9) (8)

pallarri	iringutarru	yuranga	yadni:
barlarri	iringudharu	yurhanga	yadni:
barla-rri	iri-ngu-dha-aru	yurha-nga	yadni
woman-HUM.PL	move-APPL-PRES-3.sg.ERG	man-ERG	thus

karra	pudnuru	irikanna
'garra	budnurhu	iriganha'
garra	budnu-rhu	iri-ga-nha
high	scrub-ALL	move-IMP-PL

a man bids the woman [women] to move thus: remove up to the scrub

Here we see the intransitive verb *iridhi* 'move' as plural imperative *iriganha* 'move, you lot,' being used next to its causative counterpart, *iringudhu* 'cause to move.'

Literally, this sentence reads, 'a man causes women to move/a man makes women move, thus: …' This sentence may occur in a ceremonial context in which women are excluded from some part of the proceedings. Schürmann translates *iringudhu* as 'separate,' but this is clearly not the sense of the word employed in the sentence above.

10.7.1   Causatives from derived intransitives

Derived intransitive verbs can also be made causative. In this case there is often a base form noun or adjective from which is first derived an intransitive verb, then a causative verb from that in turn. Some examples of causative verbs derived from derived intransitive verbs, that may be seen in Schürmann's vocabulary are shown in Table 10.3 at the end of this chapter. In relation to this table we may note that Adnyamathanha has *ngarla* 'plenty, much' (McEntee & McKenzie 1992: 41).

Medio-passive verbs, too, freely form transitive causative versions, as may be seen in Table 10.4 at the end of this chapter. A sentence example using the causative verb *barlagaringu-* 'raise, lift up' derived from middle verb *barlagari-* 'rise, get up, hasten' is shown here:

(10.10) Yihowanga   wilya   pallakarringutarru
(51)   Yihowanga   wilya   barlagaringudharu
         Yihowa-nga   wilya   barlaga-ri-ngu-dha-aru
         Jehovah-ERG spirit   rise-VBLZR-APPL-PRES-3.sg.ERG
         Johovah raises/lifts up the spirit

Sometimes Schürmann's dictionary offers us an adjective or a transitive verb, plus a causative verb clearly derived from an intransitivized version of the original adjective or transitive verb, but without the intransitivized version itself occurring in the dictionary. We have seen one example of this above, with the adjective *garnmi* 'encircled, enclosed,' and the causative verb *garnmiringudhu* 'encircle, enclose (=cause to be encircled, enclosed).' Given these two forms, we may predict the occurrence of a derived intransitive form *garnmiridhi** 'be encircled, enclosed.' A couple more series with gaps like this appearing in the dictionary are shown in

Table 10.5 at the end of this chapter. In this table the hypothesized derived intransitive forms are marked with asterisks.

Also in this table note that many languages have *cooking* in two versions: intransitive medio-passive, such as *the porridge is cooking,* and transitive, such as *I'm cooking the porridge.* The Barngarla causative form seen in Table 10.5 seems to be based on an intransitive version not appearing in Schürmann's vocabulary.

Occasionally causative affixes could be attached directly to a noun or adjective: based on the noun/adjective *wayi* 'fear, afraid,' for example, Schürmann has the verb *wayingudhu* 'frighten (cause to be afraid).'

10.8 Benefactive and applicative

In both Kuyani and Barngarla the causative suffixes *-ngu* and *-ngku/nggu* can signal benefactive as well as causative meanings (see Hercus 2006a for Kuyani). In both languages this suffix allows verbs, both transitive and intransitive, to take an extra object they would not otherwise be able to have.

English can do this, but in a different way: English simply adds a benefactive noun or pronoun. Looking at the verb *bake,* for example, it can be transitive with one object, as in *I'm baking a cake.* It can also be transitive with two objects, as in *I'm baking you a cake,* where the objects are both *you* and *a cake,* and where *you* is in a benefactive role: that is, it stands for someone who is benefiting from the event. In Barngarla, on the other hand, no extra pronoun need be added, but the suffix *-ngu* attached to a verb may signal that the action is being performed for the benefit of someone, stated or unstated.

10.8.1 Benefactive

Many of the verbs in Schürmann's vocabulary with *-ngu* added to them start out transitive, but going by their translations clearly do not end up being causative. They are almost certainly benefactive or applicative,[19] but their meanings, as benefactives, are elusive because of the very few sentence examples Schürmann provides, without which we are unlikely to be able to fully understand how they

---

[19] See Section 10.8.2 below.

work. Two sentence examples containing benefactive verbs illustrate the pair *irradha* 'keep off, defend, protect,' and *irrangudhu* 'protect, defend, claim.' The difference in meaning here is not causative. For the sake of comparison, two sentences are presented below to illustrate the verb *irradha* as it occurs *without* benefactive marking:

(10.11) ngarrinyelbo ninna iratanna
(7) ngarinyarlbu nhina irradhanha
    ngarinyarlbu nhina irra-dha-nha
    we   you   protect-PRES-2,3.pl

we will defend you

In this transitive sentence the object is *nhina* 'you,' the person being protected from some threat.

(10.12) kutyu yurarringe   iratanna
(7)   gudyu yurharringi   irradhanha
        gudyu yurha-rri-ngi   irra-dha-nha
        other man-HUM.PL-ERG   protect-PRES-2,3.pl

the other men keep us off

This sentence is also transitive, we can tell this by the ergative marking on the subject noun; but the object is not stated. Here *us* is apparently an object (we only know this from Schürmann's translation), but rather than being the person or thing protected, *us* constitutes a threat.

Now look at the same verb, with benefactive *(-ngu)* marking:

(10.13) mundulturringe   irangutanna   yerta
(7-8)   munduldurringi   irrangudhanha   yarda
        munduldu-rri-ngi   irra-ngu-dha-nha   yarda
        European-HUM.PL-ERG   protect-APPL-PRES-2,3.pl   land

the Europeans protect or claim the country

Adnyamathanha has *yarta* 'ground' (McEntee & McKenzie 1992: 93). In this sentence the stated object is again the thing being protected, *yarda* 'land,' but benefactive marking tells us that it is being protected for someone's benefit; in this case for the benefit of the people performing acts that constitute 'protection;' that is, keeping others off it. The same consideration applies in the next sentence:

(10.14) ngaitye karnko kutta irangukka
(7) ngadyi garngu guda irranguga
ngadyi garngu guda irra-ngu-ga
my house NEG defend-APPL-IMP

my house do not defend (= don't keep other people away from it)

A likely scenario in which this sentence was uttered, is one in which some Barngarla people had formed a relationship with Schürmann, and were keeping the material benefits accruing from that relationship for themselves, that is, away from other people. Again, the beneficiaries of this act of 'protecting' (that is, keeping other people away from Schürmann's house, and hence away from closer association with him and his goods) were those who were doing the protecting.

Some other verbs with possible benefactive derivation are listed below. We have only Schürmann's translations to go by, so this interpretation must be tentative at this stage:

gamadha *tell, intercede for, ask* gamangudhu *invite*
mirlidhi *do, make, dig up* mirlingudhu *make, create*
wanggadha *say, speak, talk* wangangudhu *tell, inform*
minadha₁ *walk in a stooping posture, creep along, steal upon game* minangudhu₁ *watch a bird or animal*
minadha₂ *take away unseen, steal* minangudhu₂ *hide, conceal*

Schürmann has *minnata* 'walk in a stooping posture' etc, as well as *menata* 'steal.' These could contain different roots, but as both meanings have to do with visibility or anti-visibility (concealment), it is likely that they are both based on the root *mina* 'eye,' in which case they are different sense meanings of the same verb. On this see also comments in Section 7.5.10.

10.8.2 Applicative

While *inviting*, as seen in the table above, is a kind of *telling* with a beneficiary; and while *informing* is a kind of *talking* with a beneficiary; and while *creating* could be a kind of *making* with a beneficiary; *watching a bird or animal* could be *stalking* with a beneficiary (the hunter), or it could be *stalking* with a victim (the bird or animal). That is to say that verbs marked with *-ngu* could code someone as either a beneficiary, or as a person affected in some other way by the action of the verb. So *minangudhu₂* 'hide, conceal,' seen above in Section 10.8.1, could code for a beneficiary, the person who is to benefit by concealment, or a victim, someone or some animal who is disadvantaged, inconvenienced or threatened by the concealment. This derivational way of signalling the presence of objects involved or affected, for good or ill, by an action, is called APPLICATIVE; and this is what we could be seeing in some of the transitive verbs derived by *-ngu/-nggu* in Schürmann's vocabulary.

We have already seen an applicative construction in Section 7.3.1 above: the sentence example in question is repeated here:

(10.15 (=7.2)) (11)

maii	kaltanyilbellinge	ngai	yeringumatta
mayi	garldanyilbilingi	ngayi	yaringumadha
mayi	garldanyi-lbili-ngi	ngayi	yari-ngu-ma-dha
food	begging-DU-ERG	I/me	greedy-APPL-2,3.du-PRES

the two beggars ask me for food

For discussion of this sentence see Section 7.3.1. For now, we need only note that the applicative morpheme *-ngu-* seen here has derived a transitive verb with two objects: 'crave, require [OBJECT 1] from [OBJECT 2],' from an adjective *yari* 'greedy.' The two objects in this example are *mayi* 'food,' and *ngayi* 'me.'

Other likely candidates for applicative readings are the following:

ilgadha *look askance, scowl*	ilgaringudhu *envy*
garldiridhi *be clamorous, beg*	garldiringudhu *ask, desire, want*
yari (adj) *greedy, stingy*	yaringudhu *crave, ask, beg*

The verb *ilgadha* has an intransitive meaning, and the transitive derivation *ilgaringudhu* is based on an intransitive form derived by *-ri*. Here *envying* appears to be a kind of *scowling* directed at a highly salient object (the person envied); and the kind of *wanting* depicted here by *garldiringudhu* is *begging* with respect to a specific goal or objective. *Begging (yaringudhu)* in Barngarla is *being greedy or stingy*, also with respect to a specific goal or adjective. The Barngarla verb *garldi-* 'be clamorous' is clearly related to the verb *garla-* 'call out' seen in Section 10.2.1.

10.8.3   *ng ~ ngk* alternation

Note the stem *wanga-ngu-* 'tell, inform' in the table in Section 10.8.1 above, rather than expected **wangga-ngu-*. Simpson & Hercus (2004: 190) cite *wangu-ngu-* 'tell somebody' in Adnyamathanha as an instance of a velar nasal-stop cluster *(*ngk)* reduced to a nasal under nasal-cluster dissimilation, but the outcome here is assimilation to the nasal in the following syllable, not dissimilation. For Adnyamathanha McEntee & McKenzie (1992: 107-108) have *wangka-* 'speak, talk,' *wangka-nga-* 'tell,' and *wangngu-* (sic) 'talk, tell.' Schebeck (1974: 17, 28), with indeterminate glossing, has *wangkatyu-angu* '(he) would say/speak,' *wangungathu-angu* 'I would say/speak,' and *wangka-angkata* 'I have explained.' From this it would appear that Adnyamathanha has both stems *wangka-nga-* and *wangu-* for 'tell,' and therefore *wangu-ngu-* with benefactive or other applicative derivation is likely. It is not uncommon for words or affixes marking causativity to be used as well to signal benefactive and other applicative meanings. On this see, eg., Shibatani & Pardeshi (2002).

In Section 10.4.2 above we encountered an alternation between the verb root *nhunggu-* 'give' and the root of its derived reciprocal counterpart *nhungu-* 'exchange'; and in Section 10.7 above we saw that the causative suffix occurs as both *-ngu* and *-nggu*. These phenomena are not unrelated: in Section 12.5.2 we will see that the causative suffix is transparently derived historically from the verb meaning 'give,' in both of its root forms *nhungu-* and *nhunggu-*.

It is likely that in Barngarla, as in other Thura-Yura languages, the phonemes *ng* and *ngk* were in free variation in a some contexts.

BASE	DERIVED WITH -*i*/-*u*	DERIVED WITH -*ri*	DERIVED WITH -(*r*)*mi*
binyi *pain*	binyidhi *be painful*	binyiridhi *feel pain*	
yalygu *together*	yalygudhu *mixing*	yalyguridhi *assemble, gather*	
wilburlu *remote*		wilburlaridhi *being distant*	wilburlunidhi *being distant*
		bundhuraridhi *blow with the mouth*	bundhunidhi *blow with the mouth*
munu-munu *at once*	munu-munidhi *be tired of (something)*	munu-muniridhi *be tired of (something)*	
ngunha *yonder*	ngunhidhi *motion with the hand, beckon*	ngunhiridhi *show with the hand, count*	
ngubi *darkness*		nguburuburidhi *be pitch dark*	ngubinidhi *be dark*
barlbara *dusty*		barlbaridhi *feel itchy*	barlbanidhi *be itchy*
yuga *dark, black*		yugiridhi *to shine black*	yuganidhi *become black*
munduldu *European*	munduldidhi *live in a European manner*	mundulduridhi *live in a European manner*	

Table 10.1: Multiple intransitive derivations

yuwadha *stand*	yuwangudhu *raise, erect (=cause (someone/something) to stand)*
warnidhi *fall*	warningudhu *let fall, throw down, drop (=cause to fall)*
iridhi *move, be moving*	iringudhu *cause (someone/something) to move*
gurrugudhu *be giddy, stupid*	gurrugungudhu *make giddy, confound (=cause to become giddy)*
mangarlidhi *be friendly*	mangarlingudhu *make peace, pacify (=cause to be friendly)*
murriridhi *be well*	murriringudhu *make well, amend (=cause to become well)*
ngamadha *go, come, run*	ngamangudhu *make come, fetch (=cause to come)*
badnadha *go*	badnanggudhu *send (=cause to go)*
budhudhu *ache*	budhunggudhu *make (something) ache*

Table 10.2: Intransitive verbs with their causative counterparts

BASE	DERIVED INTRANSITIVE	CAUSATIVE
mapara *dirty*	maparnidhi *be dirty*	maparningudhu *make dirty (=cause someone/something to be dirty)*
birrgi-birrgi *bits & pieces*	birrgi-birrgiridhi *crumble/fall to pieces*	birrgi-birrgiringudhu *(someone) break (something) into pieces*
balbara *dusty*	balbaridhi *be itchy, uncomfortable*	balbaringudhu *make dusty, dirty*
bilara *thin, sparse*	bilaridhi *be sparse, scattered*	bilaringudhu *make scarce, consume*
irri *clean*	irrinidhi *be clean*	irriningudhu *make clean, purify*
gaga *head*	gaganidhi *rise, come up, grow*	gaganingudhu *raise, rear, make grow*
wagari *asunder, in pieces*	wagaridhi *break, fall asunder*	wagaringudhu *tear, break*
galgara *narrow, close*	galgaridhi *draw close together*	galgaringudhu *close up, shut in*
ngarla *much, many*	ngarlanidhi *become large, grow*	ngarlaningudhu *make grow, increase*

Table 10.3: Causative verbs from derived intransitives

INTRANSITIVE		CAUSATIVE	
mirrgaridhi	*be startled*	mirrgaringudhu	*surprise, frighten*
balgiridhi	*crack, break, become loose*	balgiringudhu	*crack, break, as an egg*
barlagaridhi	*rise, get up, hasten*	barlagaringudhu	*raise*
barlaridhi	*shine, be lighted, enlightened*	barlaringudhu	*enlighten, instruct, inform*
biyi-biyiridhi	*blush, be shy, ashamed*	biyi-biyiringudhu	*make ashamed, say things to blush at*
gudliridhi	*be silent, sullen*	gudliringudhu	*make silent, quiet*

Table 10.4: Causative verbs from medio-passives

	DERIVED INTRANSITIVE	CAUSATIVE
ADJECTIVE: garnmi *enclosed*	garnmiridhi* *be enclosed*	garnmiringudhu *enclose*
ADJECTIVE: idla *light coloured*	idlanidhi* *be clean, light-coloured*	idlaningudhu *clean, wash*
TRANS VERB: gambadha *cook*	gambaridhi* *cook*	gambaringudhu *burn*

Table 10.5: Hypothesized derived intransitive verbs

Eleven: Non-finite verbs

Schürmann presents a set of non-finite verb forms, but with little by way of illustration as to show how they are used. He distinguishes infinitive moods, gerunds and participles as follows; with his spelling and translations:

Infinitives:

    ngukayu/ngukayi *to go*   wittiyi *to spear*

    ngukayuru *for to go*   wittiyuru *for to spear*

Gerunds:

    ngukantanga *in going*   wittintingi *in spearing*

    ngukanturlungu *in or during going*   wittinturlungu *during spearing*

    ngukaintyaranga *for going, on account of going*   wittintyaranga *for, on account of spearing*

         wittilidni *spearing*

         wittilambo *spearing*

Participle:

    ngukanyalla —   wittinyalla *spearing*

These forms take no tense endings, which is what is meant by the term 'non-finite.' Some clearly display vowel harmony, while others just as clearly resist it. About most of them we have no information whatsoever: only two of these suffixes are illustrated in any detail in Schürmann's grammar and vocabulary.

11.1 Infinitives

Although I have not found any verbs ending in *-yu* or *-yi* in Schürmann's grammar or dictionary, some there exhibit an infinitival ending he spells *-yuru*, which is likely to be phonemic *-yurhu*, containing the same PURPOSIVE suffix *-rhu* that is seen on nouns at Section 7.4.3. This shape is therefore likely to be composed of the suffix *-yu* seen in the table above, plus the PURPOSIVE suffix *-rhu*. The ending *-yurhu* has INTENTION as an important part of its meaning. It is not effected by vowel harmony. It forms verbs with non-finite meanings, such as the following:

(11.1) irkelliyulluru   ngalguyurungkalli?
(86)   irrgirliyurluru   ngalguyurhunggarli?
       irrgirli-yurluru   ngalgu-yurhu-nggarli
       salt-with/as   eat-INF-INTER

is it to be eaten with salt?

This sentence contains an associative suffix or postposition *-yulluru/-yurluru* 'as, with' found in Schürmann's vocabulary but not referred to in his grammar. The suffix *-yurhu* enables the verb *ngalgu-* 'eat' to occur without tense and without any subject being stated.

Infinitives formed with *-yurhu* are used in purposive clauses where the subject of the verb marked by *-yurhu* is not the same person (or people) as those who want the event to occur. Observe the following two sentences:

(11.2) (g19)

ngannaru	ngai	kapmarra	ngukayuru,	ninna	ngukakka
nganharhu	ngayi	gabmarra	ngugayurhu,	nhina	ngugaga
nganha-rhu	ngayi	gabmarra	nguga-yurhu	nhina	nguga-ga
what-PURP	I	always	go-INF	you	go-IMP

why am I always to go, do thou go

In the first clause of this sentence the speaker is clearly not the person who wants to go, even though he or she is the only candidate for subject status — other people, the addressee in particular, are the ones saying he or she should go.

(11.3) (12)

kaltirritao	kaitya	ngaminge	mankoyuru
garldiridhawu	gadya	ngamingi	mankuyurhu
garldi-ri-dha-wu	gadya	ngami-ngi	manku-yurhu
cry,beg-VBLZR-PRES-3.sg.NOM	child	mother-ERG	take-INF

the child cries for the mother to take it

In this sentence *ngami* 'mother' is the subject of the verb *manku-* 'take,' as is shown by her ergative case-marking. However she is not the person wanting or intending to take the child: if she were, desiderative morphology is available more clearly to signal this meaning (see Section 5.6), as *ngamingi mankungaru* 'the mother wants to take it.' The suffix *-yurhu* in both the above sentences is present when an act or event is being intended by someone other than the person who is to perform the act.

A third use of the suffix *-yurhu* is to mark purposive clauses; that is subordinate clauses that have the same subject as a previous clause. In effect this means that someone does something *in order to* do something further. The following two sentences are examples of this use:

(11.4)	pallakarritao	yura	padnayuru
(51)	barlagaridhawu	yurha	badnayurhu
	barlaga-ri-dha-wu	yurha	badna-yurhu
	rise-VBLZR-PRES-3.sg.NOM	man	go-INF

the man hastens to go

Here a man (1) rises, (2) in order to go, or rises with the intention of going.

The following example presents some problems in interpretation; Schürmann has left us no gloss for it, so the gloss here is my own. I have added punctuation in an effort to render it coherent:

(11.5) (75)

Yumbalta	kanti	wittit atto	worna	kappariuru
Yumbalda	gandhi	wididhadhu	warna	gabariyurhu.
Yumbalda	gandhi	widi-dha-adhu	warna	gaba-ri-yurhu
NAME	thigh	spear-PRES-1.sg.ERG	stomach	quiet-VBLZR-INF

kutta	wittinyanna	worna	paityannitao
Kuda	widin(d)yanha.	Warna	badyanidhawu.
guda	widi-n(d)ya-nha	warna	badya-ni-dha-wu
not	spear-PERF-2,3.pl	stomach	angry-VBLZR-PRES-3.sg.NOM

I will spear Yumbalta in the thigh in order to be appeased. They have/ ?had not speared him. He is angry.

This example seems to consist of three distinct predications, each with its own subject: 1st singular in the first sentence, 3rd plural in the second, and 3rd singular in the third. The word that Schürmann here spells *wittinyanna* may be a mis-spelling of, or a regional variant upon *wittintyanna/widindyanha* 'they have speared,' or it may be a pluperfect form (see Section 5.10). Adnyamathanha has *anthi* 'thigh' (Tunstill 2004: 420), and *warna* 'inside' (McEntee & McKenzie 1992: 109), which may correspond to the Barngarla word for 'stomach.' Like *ngali* 'liver,' *warna* 'stomach' occurs in a number of predicates denoting emotions and sensations: here we see two: *warna gaba-ri-* 'be appeased, be reconciled,' and *warna badya-ni-* 'feel anger.' The pattern here is the same as that of the sentence above it: the subject (1) spears someone, (2) in order to be appeased.

11.2 Gerunds

Schürmann lists five gerund shapes, but we have information about only one of them. Two of the shapes show a segment -*ntV*-, and two show a segment -*ngV*. This last is almost certainly a locative suffix with subordinating function, as seen in Section 7.3.5, where locative shapes are used to mark clauses that state the background or reason for some event or action that happens in an associated main clause. The shape -*ntV*- in one form or another is a common Thura-Yura verbal ending. Kuyani has a verbal ending -*nta* which appears to be used to join two verbs occurring together to depict a single event (Hercus 2006c).

The gerund ending we have good sentence examples for is -*ndyara*-. This shape is in turn always suffixed by either the locative morpheme -*nga*, or once by a shape -*nya* which might function to mark a gerund with rather more participial force than the other form. These endings mark verbs in subordinate clauses: that is, in clauses that tell us the background, the conditions, or the context of some other statement, which constitutes a main clause. The following Barngarla examples show their subordinate clauses within square brackets. Most of Schürmann's examples offer us subordinate clauses that state a reason for, or a cause of the event depicted in the main clause. These are as follows:

(11.6a) (12)

yurti	kammirriti	gadla	kundaintyaranga
yurdi	gamiridhi	gardla	gurndandyaranga
yurdi	gami-ri-dhi	[gardla	gurnda-ndyara-nga]
arm	ache-VBLZR-PRES	[fire/wood	hit-GER-LOC]

the arm aches [by beating the wood]

(11.6b) (7)

innelli	yura	ngukatao	wittintyaranya
inhirli	yurha	ngugadhawu	widhindyaranya
inhirli	yurha	nguga-dha-wu	[widhi-ndyara-nya]
tired	man	go-PRES-3.sg.NOM	[dig/stake-GER-?PPL]

a man becomes tired [by digging]

(11.6c) (23)

kakka	kurrukkutu	wanggaintyaranga
gaga	gurrugudhu	wanggandyaranga
gaga	gurrugu-dhu	[wangga-ndyara-nga]
head	be.giddy-PRES	[speak-GER-LOC]

my head becomes giddy [by talking]

(11.6d) (7)

kutyu	yurarringe	iratanna	'winni winni'
gudyu	yurharringi	irradhanha	'wini wini'
gudyu	yurha-rri-ngi	irra-dha-nha	[wini wini
other	man-HUM.PL-ERG	protect-PRES-2,3.pl	[wini wini

wanggaintyaranga

wanggandyaranga

wangga-ndyara-nga]

speak-GER-LOC]

the other men keep us off [by saying 'wini wini']

(11.6e) (11)

kalkarrimatta	ngaitye	pinkalbelli	warra
galgarimadha	ngadyi	birngalbili	warra
galga-ri-ma-dha	ngadyi	birnga-lbili	[warra
tremble-VBLZR-2,3.du-PRES	my	hip-DU	[far

ngukaintyaranga

ngugandyaranga

nguga-ndyara-nga]

go-GER-LOC]

my hips ache [from travelling far]

In (11.6a) the noun *gardla* 'fire' has an extended meaning as 'piece of wood,' that is, 'firewood.' Sentence (11.6b) shows the only instance of the ending *-ndyara-nya* occurring in Schürmann's vocabulary. Adnyamathanha has a verb *withi-* 'spear, stake' (that is, impale with a stick into the ground) (McEntee & McKenzie 1992: 121), and I will presume that this is the verb occurring here, as *widhi-*. Sentence (11.6d) is almost certainly taken from some ceremonial context. In sentence (11.6e) the noun *birnga* 'hip' is reflected in Adnyamathanha *virnkarlpu* 'hip bone' (McEntee & McKenzie 1992: 65).

As well as depicting reasons for events, subordinate clauses in Barngarla may describe the context or conditions under which the event of a main clause takes place. The following sentence shows us the context as well as the reason for the action in the main clause:

(11.7) (48)

ngupurrupurrintyaranga	gadla	kattitarru
nguburuburindyaranga	gardla	gadidharu
[nguburubu-ri-ndyara-nga]	gardla	gadi-dha-aru
[pitch.dark-VBLZR-GER-LOC]	fire	carry-PRES-3.sg.ERG

he carries a firestick [because it is pitch dark]

The verb in the subordinate clause is *nguburuburidhi* 'be pitch dark,' based on the noun *ngubi* 'darkness.' The construction of this verb is discussed in Section 10.1.2.

The following sentence is more complicated, as it shows in its subordinate clause not so much a condition, as a context or a goal for the event in the main clause:

(11.8) (54)

ninna	Adelaidiru	parrakutyungu	ngukaintyaranga
nhina	Adelaide-rhu	barragudyungu	ngugandyaranga
[nhina	Adelaide-rhu	barragudyu-ngu	nguga-ndyara-nga]
[you.sg	NAME-ALL	until-LOC	go-GER-LOC]

yalgaltanga	kanaru
Yalgaldanga	ganaru
Yalgalda-nga	gana-aru
NAME-ERG	wait-3.sg.ERG

Yalgalda may wait/ let Yalgalda wait [til you go to Adelaide]

The verb *ganaru* in the main clause is an hortative form marked for a 3rd singular ergative subject, which is the person called Yalgalda. As we saw in Section 8.1.1, a noun object of the verb *gana-* 'wait' is usually marked by the GOAL suffix *-lbu*. In this sentence Yalgalda is not waiting for a person or for a thing, but for an event that is predicted to occur in the future. For this reason the gerundive verb *ngugandyaranga* is (probably) suffixed with a locative ending in subordinating function. Note as well that even the conjunction or adverb *barragudyu* 'until' gets locative case-marking in this sentence; that is, in Barngarla the adverb/conjunction is part of the subordinate clause, not of the main clause nor interclausal.

Schürmann's vocabulary includes what looks like a subordinate clause without a main clause. In this clause the gerundive verb is *yarnbaringudhu* 'mention, speak of,' described below:

(11.9) (84)

nunno	yernbarringuntyaranga	kauo	wornitao
nhurnu	yarnbaringundyaranga	gawu	warnidhawu
[nhurnu	yarnba-ri-ngu-ndyara-nga]	gawu	warni-dha-wu
[you.sg.ERG	declare-VBLZR-APPL-GER-LOC]	water	lie-PRES-3.sg.NOM

[your mentioning of/ when you made mention of] water lying there

Clearly this utterance is taken out of some context that has not been bequeathed to us.

In one final sentence example Schürmann shows us what appears to be a negative subordinating suffix *-lla/ -rla*, attached to a gerund form, as in the following:

(11.10) (g23)

yura	ikkaintyarangalla	pony	kularabmatao
yurha	igandyarangarla	pony	gurlarhabmadhawu
[yurha	iga-ndyara-nga-rla]	pony	gurlarhabma-dha-wu
[person	sit-GER-LOC-?NEG]	pony	sweat-PRES-3.sg.NOM

the horse sweats [without any one riding him]

Adnyamathanha has *urlarha* 'shed skin, exuvia,' (McEntee & McKenzie 1992: 32) which meaning is quite close to 'sweat,' and which must correspond to Barngarla *kularra/gurlarha* 'sweat.' The Barngarla verb root *gurlarha-bma-* 'sweat' appears to include a possibly derivational, and possibly archaic morpheme *-bma* (see Section 4.1.1). The ending *-ndyara-nga-rla* may be dedicated to forming negative subordinate clauses of this sort.

Added later to his grammar, Schürmann has written the word *ngukamantyaranga*, a gerund with coding for a dual subject:

(11.11) ngukamantyaranga

(g19) ngugamandyaranga

        nguga-ma-ndyara-nga

        go- 2,3.du-GER-LOC

        both their going

11.3 Other forms

We have already seen in Section 10.6 present participles built from derived intransitive verbs. In Schürmann's vocabulary there is a single example of a verb with the participial ending *-nyalla* (possibly phonemic *-nyarla*), in a verb form given as a synonym for another expression meaning 'commanding, domineering:' *yarnba-yarnbanyarla*. There is another verb *yarnbaringudhu* 'mention, speak of' (|yarnba-ri-ngu-dhu| [declare-VBLZR-APPL-PRES]), and the participle *yarnba-yarnbanyarla* appears to be built from a reduplication of the root of this causative verb, as |yarnba-yarnba-nyarla| [declare-declare-PARTICIPLE].

There is one occurrence in Schürmann's vocabulary of a sentence example containing a verb suffixed by the gerund ending *-nta-nga (-nda-nga)*:

(11.12) (g22)

patharutye	wannintunn'ai	nuro	kanantanga
badharhudyi	warnindhunayi	nhurru	ganandanga
badharhu-dyi	warni-ndhu-na-ayi	[nhurru	gana-nda-nga]
thither-TOP	lie-CONT-PAST-1.sg.NOM	[you.sg.PATR	wait-GER$_2$-LOC]

there I remained lying, [waiting for thee]

All we can observe about the verb *ganandanga* 'waiting' here is that (1) it refers to an act occurring at the same time as the event in the main clause, (2) it has the same subject as the verb in the main clause, and (3) it shows a locative suffix in subordinating function.

Twelve: Putting words together

So far we have been able to observe some of Barngarla's basic morphology, but there is more to language than morphology. The grammar of a language includes most importantly the network of abstract relations that hold between words, that enable them to be assembled into meaningful sequences of sounds. To some extent we have been able to see how some of these networks operate in Barngarla; we have seen how words may be turned into verbs, how verbs may be made intransitive or transitive, how nouns and pronouns code for who is doing what to whom, and how things may be described one in relation to another.

Nineteenth century linguistics was interested mainly in morphology as this was the most impressive feature of Latin, Sanskrit and Homeric Greek, which were studied as exemplars of linguistic elaboration and sophistication *par excellence*. It was not until the late nineteenth century that linguists began to look seriously beyond morphology at the systems of dependencies that constitute syntax.

Nevertheless, Schürmann's vocabulary offers us examples of Barngarla sentences from which we are able to glimpse some of the syntactic relationships that hold between the different parts of utterances. A few of these phenomena will be surveyed here, not as an exhaustive account of what Schürmann has left us, but rather as a suggestion of what else we may yet be able to discover.

12.1 Using pronouns

Pronouns in Thura-Yura languages were not used nearly as frequently as they are in English (see Hercus 1999: 71 for Wirangu). As in many or even most languages, Barngarla people probably gathered who was doing what to whom most of the time from context: that is, from what was happening around them, or from what people had just been talking about. So five-syllable pronouns like *budlanbidningi* 'with them two' and *yardnagudnirhu* 'to them' were probably used only when there was ambiguity, and in order to make someone's meaning clear; and this may not have been very often. Likewise, pronouns were used quite differently from the way we use pronouns. So in English we would normally say, *go with him*, using the third person singular pronoun *him*. It would probably *not* be correct to translate this directly into Barngarla:

(12.1)   barnundyudningi   ngugaga

with.him   go-IMPERATIVE

go with him

Instead, Barngarla speakers probably used a second person dual ('you two') pronoun:

(12.2)   nhuwala   ngugamaga

nhuwala   nguga-ma-ga

you.two   go-DU-IMP

you two go / go with him

or even more likely, just a verb with dual imperative marking:

(12.3a)   ngugamaga

nguga-ma-ga

go-DU-IMP

you two go / you & him go / go with him

(12.3b) Fred   ngugamaga

Fred   nguga-ma-ga

Fred   go-DU-IMP

you & Fred go/go with Fred

Pronouns that refer specifically to certain types of kinfolk could be used on their own to denote those relationships. For example the reference of the 3rd dual pronoun *budlanbi* 'they two,' or an important part of its reference at least, was to a husband and wife. So a sentence such as the following, using the existential verb *badna-* 'go,' could be used to describe two people as being married:

(12.4)   pudlanbi   padnamatta

(g13)   budlanbi   badnamadha

budlanbi   badna-ma-dha

they.two   go-2,3.du-PRES

they two are husband and wife

12.2 Verbless sentences

Barngarla has no joining verb like the English verb *be*, although it does have a number of stance verbs. Instead Schürmann records a word *ta* (phonemic *dhaa*) that appears to function existentially in short sentences. He offers only two examples of this word:

(12.5a) innaratà

(62)   inhara   dhaa

here.it.is   CONJ

there it is

(12.5b) mantyarri   ta
(g14)   mandyarri   dhaa
        good,fresh   CONJ
        it is good or well

Adnyamathanha has a word *inhari* 'here you are,' based on *inha* 'this' (McEntee & McKenzie 1992: 21, Schebeck 1974: 12), and Schürmann's sentence example clearly contains the Barngarla equivalent of this word. Adnyamathanha also has the joining word *tha* (Schebeck 1974: 46-47). Adnyamathanha *mandha* 'fresh (of food)' (McEntee & McKenzie 1992: 79) may relate to Barngarla *mandyarri* 'good.'

Longer sentences can be constructed without verbs, and when this is done the result is an equational sentence, in which something is said to be, or to have the properties of, something else. Two examples Schürmann offers are:

(12.6) mangalla   yurarri   innamatta
(g10)   mangarla   yurharri   inhamadha
        mangarla   yurha-rri   inha-madha
        friendly   man-HUM.PL   this-PL
        friendly men (are) these

Although I have found no correspondence in other languages to Schürmann's *mangalla* 'friendly, peaceable,' I will suppose that the *ll* indicates retroflexion here, by analogy with his spelling *Parnkalla* of Barngarla. In this sentence *inhamadha* 'these' are said to be friendly men; so that in a sense, 'these = friendly men.' In the next sentence people who spoke Nhawu are described as having certain properties:

(12.7) Nauurri   irabukarri   kadla   willururri
(g10)   Nhawurri   irabugarri,   gadlha   wirlurhurri
        Nhawu-rri   ira-buga-rri   gadlha   wirlurhu-rri
        name-HUM.PL   tooth-rotten-HUM.PL   penis   long-HUM.PL
        the Nauos (are) teeth rotten and long rumped

Kuyani has *ira* 'teeth' (Hercus 2006a), and Adnyamathanha has *wirlurha* 'stripe' (McEntee & McKenzie 1992: 124), which I will take to be related to the Barngarla word meaning 'long' that Schürmann spells *willuru*. Kuyani has *kadlha* 'tail' (Hercus 2006a), and Wirangu has *galya* 'tail, penis' (Miller et al 2010: 33). Schürmann has translated this sentence with some delicacy.

12.3 Existential verbs

Schürmann lists five existential or stance verbs in Barngarla. These verbs describe in general or abstract terms the stance or posture that some entity adopts, or the vector dynamics that some entity engages in. They are used usually where English uses the existential verb *be*. Adnyamathanha too has a set of five existential verbs, with essentially the same meanings (Schebeck 1974: 54). In Barngarla these verbs are as follows:

yuwadha	*stand*	used to depict entities in a vertical position or stance
warnidhi	*fall, lie*	used to depict entities in a horizontal position
igadha	*sit*	used to depict compact or dispersed entities
badnadha	*go*	a verb of general existence, with no stance or vector dynamic involved
garhidhi	*continue*	used to depict entities in a state of motion or potential motion

Kuyani has a verb *karhi-* 'get up, stand up, come out, protrude, grow' (Hercus 2006a,b), with vectorial semantics general enough to make it suitable to be a verb of stance or posture, and with a meaning just possibly reflected in Schürmann's translation 'continue; be or exist still.' The Adnyamathanha existential equivalent of Barngarla *garhi-* is *witni-*, which Schebeck and McEntee & McKenzie (1992: 121) translate as 'go/wander around,' and this may be a good translation for Barngarla *garhi-* also.

We have already seen the verb *badna-* used as an existential verb in three previous sentence examples: (8.2b), (8.11c) and (12.4). In these sentences *badna-* is existential, it does not denote motion; rather it is used where English uses the joining verb *be* (as *is* and *are* in these sentences). Schürmann offers other sentences with existential verbs:

(12.8a)   kaya-ilka   padnatanna
(=7.26)   gayalyga   badnadhanha
(g14)   gaya-lyga   badna-dha-nha
          spear-ASSOC   go-PRES-2,3.pl

they have spears

(12.8b)   kutyo   yurarri   yarlanga   padnatanna
(g14)   gudyu   yurharri   yarlanga   badnadhanha
          gudyu   yurha-rri   yarla-nga   badna-dha-nha
          other   man-HUM.PL   hunt-LOC   go-PRES-2,3.pl

the other men are hunting

(12.8c)   ngai   kubmanna   padnata
(50)   ngayi   gubmanha   badnadha
          ngayi   gubmanha   badna-dha
          I   one/alone   go-PRES

I am alone, ie I have no relatives

The word *yarlanga* appears to be an adverb *yarla* 'hunting, chasing' inflected for locative case: in Schürmann's vocubulary it occurs as *yerla* 'hunt chase,' which may be comparable to the Adnyamathanha verb root *yurtli-* 'chase, hunt' (McEntee & McKenzie 1992: 101, Tunstill 2004: 427). In his vocabulary the sentence example given is *paru yerlanga padnata* 'to go hunting' which is phonemic *barhu yarlanga badnadha* 'going hunting,' or 'hunting.' It is not uncommon in arid Australia for hunting to be denoted by adverbs: Manyjilyjarra, for example, has *karrila* 'daytime hunting trip' and *wartilpa* 'hunting trip.'

(12.9)	pallarri	kangaranga	karitanna
(g14)	barlarri	gangarhanga	garhidhanha
	barla-rri	gangarha-nga	garhi-dha-nha
	woman-HUM.PL	grasstree.root-LOC	continue-PRES-2,3.pl

the women are among the kangara *or grass tree roots*

Schürmann's *kangara* is the edible root of the grass-tree: Wirangu has *gangurhu* 'grass seeds for making flour' (Miller et al 2010: 35), and it may be possible to imagine a phonological correspondence between these words.

12.4 Body-part nouns

Many languages, including Australian languages, have a set of nouns that are conceived of as being part of one's person, and as such, are not able to be alienated from a person.[20] Typically these are nouns that denote things like your name, your shadow, your close kin, your soul and parts of your body. When these nouns occur in a phrase with the 'owner' of the part, or more accurately with the 'whole' to which the part belongs or is attached, the owner does not receive possessive marking. This is the case in Barngarla, as the following sentences show:

(12.10a)	ngai	kakka	purarriti
(61)	ngayi	gaga	burarhidhi
	ngayi	gaga	burarhi-dhi
	I	head	ache-PRES

I have [a] head ache

---

[20] See Chappell & McGregor (eds) (1996) for this phenomenon in Australia and elsewhere.

(12.10b)	nunno	yura	kakka	puttungkutu
(62)	nhurnu	yurha	gaga	budhunggudhu
	nhurnu	yurha	gaga	budhu-nggu-dhu
	you.sg.ERG	person	head	ache-APPL-PRES

you make people['s] head ache

(12.10c)	ngai	worna	tarkalla
(62)	ngayi	warna	darrgarla
	I	stomach	hard/swollen

my stomach is hard

Schürmann has *purarra* 'weak, feeble, tired,' and Kuyani has *parawarha-* 'be crazy, have a bad head, have a headache' (Hercus 2006a). Schürmann also has *tarkalla/darrgarla* 'hard, swollen, inflamed.' Notice here the phrases *ngayi gaga* 'my head,' *yurha gaga* '(a) person's head' and *ngayi warna* 'my stomach.' Here the owner is in nominative case *(ngayi, yurha)* rather than in possessive case or with possessive marking, as could be expected otherwise. The phrase *warna darrgarla* 'hard stomach' probably refers to stubbornness, resoluteness or determination, metaphorically.

However we can also note, in sentence example (11.6e) in Section 11.2 above, the phrase *ngadyi birngalbili* 'my hips,' with the 1st singular possessive pronoun *ngadyi*. It may be that this body-part noun in this context takes a dependent noun (an 'owner' or whole) with possessive marking because here the hips are being metaphorically separated from the owner, in order to pay them special attention.

In many Australian languages kinship relations are seen, at least in some contexts, as being integral parts of one's person, and so do not receive possessive case-marking. This is not the case in Barngarla: here the 'owner' of a kin relation is marked by possessive inflection, as we have seen in *babi ngadyi* 'my father' in sentence example (8.2c), and also in sentences such as the following:

(12.11) nunko   pappi   watha
(73)   nhunku   babi   waadha
        you.POSS father   where

where is your father?

12.5 Complex predication

Compounding, by one definition, occurs when two or more words occur together to make a meaning different from either. In Schürmann's dictionary we can see a number of instances that look like complex or compounded expressions of this sort. Here we will look briefly at just three.

12.5.1 Sensation predicates

In Aboriginal culture the stomach is very often the seat of the emotions, just as the heart is in Western culture. Barngarla shows two metaphors of this sort, one based on the stomach, *warna*, and the other based on the liver, *ngali*. Schürmann's *ngalli* 'liver' is phonemic *ngali*, as Wirangu and Kuyani both have *ngalti* for this meaning, showing that the lateral is apico-alveolar. The Barngarla word *ngali* 'liver' is involved in no less than ten compound predicates denoting emotions and sensations, and another four are listed without glosses

It may not be possible at this time to know whether such expressions were phonologically compounded as two parts of a single word, or if they were phonologically distinct words that were lexically collocated. Schürmann's transcriptions are frequently inconsistent in this respect, and I will separate the compounded parts here for clarity and convenience. In the following list the simplex verb or adjective is set in front of the compounded or collocated expression:

With *ngali* 'liver'

yaldadha	?	ngali yaldadha	*feel dull or sad*
		ngali yaldadha	*rejoice, exult*
bagambidhi	*be full*	ngali bagambidhi	*relent, sympathize*
murriridhi	*be well*	ngali murriridhi	*feel well, easy*
mirrirraridhi	?	ngali mirrirraridhi	*be without feeling, merciless*
ngudharidhi	*quarrel, argue*	ngali ngudharidhi	*grieve, fret*

With *warna* 'stomach'

bagambidhi	*be full*	warna bagambidhi	*fret, grieve*
waburnidhi	*be full*	warna waburnidhi	*be satiated*
gaba	*?quiet*	warna gabaridhi	*be reconciled, appeased*
mundalya	*sweet, nice*	warna mundalyidhi	*feel glad, merry*
badya	*anger*	warna badyanidhi	*feel anger*
gularidhi	*crack, break*	warna gularidhi	*be frightened, startled*

Some of these compounds are likely to be synonymous, such as *waburnidhi* 'be full' and *warna waburnidhi* 'be satiated.' Notice how the verb *bagambidhi* 'be full' is able to contribute two quite distinct meanings, depending upon whether it is collocated with *warna* or *ngali*. Schürmann has no distinct entry for the verb or verbs *yaltata/yaldadha*, but it is probable that the medial lateral-stop cluster occurs at different places of articulation in each predicate, to signal two distinct verbs, as, for example, *yaldadha/yarldadha/yaldhadha*.

12.5.2 *Nhunggudhu* as causative

The verb *nhunggudhu* 'give' appears in a number of complex predicates, preceded by an initial element that is a noun, a verb or an adverb (and presumably adjectives are not barred from such constructions). The verb *nhunggudhu* appears to contribute applicative or at least causative meanings to these expressions. They are reasonably frequent in the dictionary. Some examples are shown in Table 12.1 at the end of this chapter. In relation to this table, note that Adnyamathanha has *wandha-* 'leave alone, relinquish' (McEntee & McKenzie 1992: 112), and *ngarha* 'untruth, lie' (Tunstill 2004: 424).

Expressions like *wayi nhunggudhu* 'frighten' clearly reveal the causative function of the verb *nhunggudhu* in many of these predicates. From this it is reasonable to suppose that the northern Thura-Yura causative affix *-nggu/ngu* has developed as an abbreviation of the stem *nhungku-*, with the initial CV sequence dropped in a manner characteristic of Thura-Yura elision generally.

12.6 Negation

Barngarla verbs are negated quite simply, by having the word *guda* set in front of them. We have already encountered examples of this construction in sentence examples (7.18b, 10.4, 10.13) and (11.5). A couple more from Schürmann's vocabulary are shown below:

(12.12)	metye	yurringi	kutta	battarritao
(2)	midyi	yurhingi	guda	badharidhawu
	midyi	yurhi-ngi	guda	badha-ri-dha-wu
	name	ear-LOC	NEG	remain-VBLZR-PRES-3.sg.NOM

the name remains not in the ear = I have forgot it

Schürmann has transitive *battata/badadha* 'drive away, scare off,' and intransitive *battabattarriti/badabadaridhi* 'disperse.' The meaning of the verb root he spells *batta-* 'remain' in the example above clearly has to do with permanence. This root could be homophonous with the root meaning 'drive away,' or it could be a differently shaped root altogether, either *barta-* or *badha-* (as represented here).

Imperative utterances are also negated by having *guda* set in front of them:

(12.13)	kalya	kutta	kundakka
(12)	galya	guda	gurndaga
	galya	guda	gurnda-ga
	INTRJCT	NEG	hit-IMP

don't strike, I say

Here the word *galya* is an interjection of the sort indicated by Schürmann in this example.

ngarha *error, deception, falsehood*	ngarha nhunggudhu *deceive, tantalize, promise and not give*
wayi *fear*	wayi nhunggudhu *frighten, make afraid*
wandhadha *leave alone*	wandha nhunggudhu *leave alone, refuse*
ganya *stone*	ganya nhunggudhu *detain by force, prevent*
madlu *shade*	madlu nhunggudhu *kill, destroy life*
maldi *darkness, night*	maldi nhunggudhu *kill, send out of the world*
mulga *tear, cry, lamentation*	mulga nhunggudhu *hold a lamentation*

Table 12.1: Applicative function of *nhunggudhu* 'give'

Thirteen: Prospect

This commentary is just that: it is intended as an exegesis of the first section of Schürmann's Barngarla vocabulary, and no more. It certainly does not pretend to encompass all that we are able to know or find out about Barngarla grammar.

For example, the vocabulary is full of untranslated sentence examples, added from Schürmann's manuscript notes by Schürmann himself in or about 1884. As an example of such a sentence, note the following, appearing under a lemma *pulyallana* on page 60, and without a gloss:

> *Pulyallana, Kukata yerkulludni yura, yakkara mapparrintyarru, pardnüntyuru pallarri yunduntyanna kanyannityanna*

This passage must refer to the Barngarla culture hero Pulyállana (possibly phonemic Bulyárlanha) whose story is outlined in Schürmann (1846/2009: 238-239)), and who appears to be portrayed here as a Kukarta ancestor *(Kukarta yarrguludni yurha)* who had two wives (note *barlarri* 'women' here). However we cannot at this stage say much more about it.

Close examination of the vocabulary section itself would doubtlessly enhance our understanding in many ways. Examination of Moonie Davis' recorded material referred to in Section 1.3 could also advance our knowledge considerably, and complement the information Schürmann has left us.

As well, and very importantly, a greater understanding of the grammar and lexicon of Adnyamathanha, still a living language, could be of inestimable assistance in clarifying aspects of Barngarla grammar, and of the grammar of other Thura-Yura languages, and in extending our knowledge of them. The full and careful documentation of Adnyamathanha must now be an urgent priority in any programme of language reclamation envisaged in South Australia.

Despite its brevity, and despite the ongoing gaps in our knowledge, Schürmann's grammar, as well as his vocabulary, continues to be an indispensable starting point for the further exploration of the Barngarla language.

Appendix: The name *Barngarla*

The phonological shape of the language name Schürmann transcribed as *Parnkalla* may be checked against recent recordings of this word. In Adnyamathanha the word occurs as *Varngarla* (Mcentee & McKenzie 1992: 56) showing retroflex nasal and lateral, although in 1960 O'Grady spelled the name *Pankarla*, (O'Grady 2001: 292), a representation he must have checked with Hale, who worked with Barngarla man Harry Crawford at Iron Knob on that occasion. Hercus & White (1973: 61) recorded the name as *Baŋgaḻa*, showing a velar nasal, as do maps drawn by Berndt and Tindale (reproduced in Hercus & Simpson 2001: 268-269) which have *Banggala* and *Baŋgaḻa* respectively. Tindale appears to have considered that *Banggala* was a valid alternative pronunciation,[21] and Hercus (1999: 12) treats this word as a northern dialect label. In view of Mcentee & McKenzie's *Varngarla*, and Crawford's *Pankarla*, a form *Banggarla* or something like it may have been a northern dialectal variant, or even an exonymic pronunciation.

Hercus & Simpson (2001: 271) discuss a possible etymology for the word *Barngarla*, incorporating *kalla* 'voice, speech,' probably phonemic *garla*, corresponding to archaic Adnymathanha *arlda* 'language.' The nineteenth century settler A N Swiss spelled the word *Parnkulta* in a letter to R H Mathews (cited in Hercus & Simpson 2001: 271), supporting both the retroflex place of the nasal, and their proposed etymology. The language name was likely to have been phonemic /parnkarla/, at least around Port Lincoln. Swiss' spelling *Parnkulta* makes

---

[21] South Australian Museum archives at <http://archives.samuseum.sa.gov.au/tindaletribes/pangkala.htm>.

it fairly certain that this label variant, as *Barnkarlda*, reflects archaic Adnyamathanha *arlda* 'language' and Barngarla *garla*, or reconstructable early Thura-Yura **karlta* 'language.'

Simpson and Hercus (2001: 271, fn 11) point out that an initial element *parn* would be phonotactically illegal in Barngarla, so we may wish to look for an initial element *parnga* that might have formed *parnga-garla** → *parngarla*. The Barngarla word *parnga* probably meant 'hot, heat' or similar. Schürmann lists a verb *parnkata*, phonemic *barngadha*, without a gloss but with a sentence example: *ngalli parnkata/parnkalliti bukarranga* 'to be hot.' The verb *parnkata* occurs under another lemma with another sentence example, *ngalli parnkata*, again without a gloss. Under the lemma *parnkata* it looks as if an original printed sentence example *ngalli parnkata* has been overwritten by hand to read *ngalli parnkalliti bukarranga*. This is problematic in itself, as *parnkalliti* is phonemic *barngarlidhi*, that is, a verb derived by regular process from the noun *barngarla* with the present-tense ending *-dhi*. This overwriting (possibly by Tindale) may have been occasioned by mistaken reference to, or confusion with the preceding lemma, which is *parnkalliti* 'to be Parnkalla, to speak the Parnkalla language.' The original sentence example could possibly be more reliable as an indication of the meaning of the verb *parnkata*. The compounded use of the word *ngali* 'liver' is discussed above in Section 12.5.1. The word *bukarra* is phonemic *bugara* 'fine weather, hot weather,' marked for locative case with *-nga* (cf Wirangu *bugara* 'hot weather' (Miller et al 2010: 12)). It appears, then, that the noun *ngali* 'liver' serves to identify or classify verbs as sensation predicates, and the inflected word *bukarranga* 'in hot weather' is given here to indicate the kind of sensation that may be denoted by the predicate as a whole.

Schürmann also lists the word *parnkumbu* as *crepitus ventri* (=*crepitus ventris*), literally 'creaking or popping noises of the stomach,' but usually denoting flatulence, hence Schürmann's Latin. Barngarla *gumbu* is 'urine,' and a compounded word *parnga-gumbu** → *parngumbu*, literally 'hot urine' would be reasonable for the denotation of the diarrhoea that may accompany stomach infection, and by extension or association to intestinal gas.

If the above conjectures are not fatuous, the etymology of the language name *Barngarla* may be *barnga garla* 'hot speech.' This expression would clearly be a metaphor and as such unfortunately may tell us nothing at all about its social or historical significance.

References

Amery, Robert, 2016, Warrabarna Kaurna! Reclaiming an Australian language. Adelaide: University of Adelaide Press.

Amery, Robert, & Jane Simpson, 2013, *Kulurdu marni ngathaitya! A Kaurna learner's guide*. Adelaide: Wakefield Press.

Chappell, Hillary, & William B McGregor (eds), 1996, *The grammar of inalienability: a typological perspective on body-part terms and the part-whole relation*. Berlin: Mouton de Gruyter.

Clendon, Mark, 2006, 'Re-assessing Australia's linguistic prehistory.' *Current Anthropology*, 47(1): 39-62.

Clendon, Mark, 2011, *Expert linguistic report in relation to the Yilka native title determination application*. Perth: Central Desert Native Title Services Ltd.

Clendon, Mark, 2014, *Worrorra: a language of the north-west Kimberley coast*. Adelaide: University of Adelaide Press.

Dediu, Dan, & Stephen Levinson, 2013, 'On the antiquity of language: the reinterpretation of Neandertal linguistic capacities and its consequences.' *Frontiers in Psychology*, 5/7/13. doi: 10.3389/fpsyg.2013.00397.

Dixon, R M W, 2002, *Australian languages: their nature and development*. Cambridge: Cambridge University Press.

Garrett, Andrew, 1990, 'The origin of NP split ergativity.' *Language* 66(2): 261-296.

Hale, Kenneth, 1982, 'Some essential features of Warlpiri verbal clauses.' In S Swartz (ed), *Papers in Warlpiri grammar in memory of Lothar Jagst*. Work Papers of SIL-AAB, Series A Vol 6. Darwin: Summer Institute of Linguistics (217-315).

Hercus, Luise, 1965, Parnkalla and Kokatha language elicitation with Moonie Davis (Point Pearce). Audiotape, Canberra, AIATSIS. Field recording no 21/17, archive item no HERCUS_Lo8-000994B.

Hercus, Luise, 1966, Vocabulary and sentence elicitation in Parnkalla with Moonie Davis (Andamooka). Audiotape, Canberra, AIATSIS. Field recording no FT 34, archive item nos HERCUS_L16-002020B, -002021A

Hercus, Luise, 1992, *A Nukunu dictionary.* Canberra: The Author.

Hercus, Luise, 1999, *A grammar of the Wirangu language from the west coast of South Australia.* Canberra: Pacific Linguistics C-150.

Hercus, Luise, 2006a, Preliminary Kuyani vocabulary. Ms.

Hercus, Luise, 2006b, Preliminary English – Kuyani finder list. Ms.

Hercus, Luise, 2006c, Notes for tape 466. Ms.

(The above three references are included in 71 hours of material in Kuyani and other languages stored in Canberra at AIATSIS as Collection no HERCUS L_27, Archive nos 004293-004328.)

Hercus, Luise, & Jane Simpson, 2001, 'The tragedy of Nauo.' In J Simpson, D Nash, M Laughren, P Austin & B Alpher (eds), *Forty years on: Ken Hale and Australian languages.* Canberra: Pacific Linguistics (263-290).

Hercus, Luise A, & Isobel M White, 1973, 'Perception of kinship structure reflected in the Adnjamathanha pronouns.' In *Papers in Australian linguistics no. 6.* Canberra: Pacific Linguistics A-36 (47-75).

Hylton, Jane, 2012, *South Australia illustrated: colonial painting in the land of promise.* Adelaide: Art Gallery of South Australia.

Marsh, James, 1992 *Martu Wangka—English Dictionary.* Darwin: Summer Institute of Linguistics.

McEntee, J, & P McKenzie, 1992, AḊŇA-MAṮ-ŇA *English dictionary.* Adelaide: The Authors.

McConvell, Patrick & Barry Alpher, 2002, 'On the Omaha trail in Australia: tracking skewing from east to west.' *Anthropological Forum* 12: 159-175.

Miller, G, L Hercus, P Monaghan & P Naessan, 2010, *A dictionary of the Wirangu language of the far west coast of South Australia.* Adelaide: Tjutjunaku Worka Tjuta & the University of Adelaide.

O'Grady, Geoff, 1988, Pankarla wordlist. AIATSIS identifier code AILEC 0077. Ms.

O'Grady, Geoff, 2001, 'Two southern Australian vocabularies: Parnkalla (Barngarla) and Karlamayi.' In J Simpson, D Nash, M Laughren, P Austin & B Alpher (eds), *Forty years on: Ken Hale and Australian languages.* Canberra: Pacific Linguistics (291-303).

O'Grady, G, H Hale, N Tindale, B Schebeck, P Austin & J McEntee, nd, *Adnyamathanha wordlist.* Aboriginal Studies Electronic Data Archive (ASEDA) document 0107. Canberra: Australian Institute of Aboriginal & Torres Strait Islander Studies.

Platt, John, 1967, 'The Kukata—Kukatja distinction.' *Oceania* 38(1): 61-64.

Platt, John, 1972, *An outline grammar of the Gugada dialect: South Australia.* Canberra: AIAS. Australian Aboriginal Studies no 48, Linguistic Series no 20.

Schebeck, Bernhard, 1973, 'The Adnjamathanha personal pronoun and the 'Wailpi' kinship system.' In *Papers in Australian linguistics no 6.* Canberra: Pacific Linguistics A-36 (1-45).

Schebeck, Bernhard, 1974, *Texts on the social system of the Aḏn̩yamaṯana people with grammatical notes.* Canberra: Pacific Linguistics D-21.

Schürmann, Clamor, 1844, *A vocabulary of the Parnkalla language spoken by the natives inhabiting the western shores of Spencer's Gulf, to which is prefixed a collection of grammatical rules, hitherto ascertained.* Adelaide: George Dehane.

Schürmann, Clamor, 1846 [1879], [2009], *The Aboriginal tribes of Port Lincoln in South Australia: their mode of life, manners, customs, etc.* Adelaide: George Dehane. Reprinted in 1879 in *The Native Tribes of South Australia*, Adelaide: E S Wigg & Son, and in a new edition published in 2009 by the Friends of the State Library of South Australia (207-251).

Schürmann, C, J Simpson, G O'Grady & A Harvey, 1993, [1844], *A vocabulary of the Parnkalla language.* Aboriginal Studies Electronic Data Archive (ASEDA) document 0256. Version dated 17/1/93. Canberra: Australian Institute of Aboriginal & Torres Strait Islander Studies.

Schurmann, Edwin, 1987, *I'd rather dig potatoes: Clamor Schurmann and the Aborigines of South Australia, 1838-1853*. Adelaide: Lutheran Publishing House.

Shibatani, M, & P Pardeshi, 2002, 'The causative continuum.' In M Shibatani (ed), *The grammar of causation and interpersonal manipulation*. Amsterdam: John Benjamins (85-126).

Silverstein, Michael, 1976, 'Hierarchy of features and ergativity.' In R M W Dixon (ed), *Grammatical categories in Australian languages*. Canberra: Australian Institute of Aboriginal Studies (112-171).

Simpson, Jane, 1995, 'Making sense of the words in old wordlists.' In N Thieberger (ed), *Paper and talk: a manual for reconstituting materials in Australian indigenous languages from historical sources*. Canberra: Aboriginal Studies Press.

Simpson, J, & L Hercus, 2004, 'Thura-Yura as a subgroup.' In C Bowern & H Koch (eds), *Australian languages: classification and the comparative method*. Amsterdam: John Benjamins.

Teichelmann, C G, 1857, *Dictionary of the Adelaide dialect*. MS 4vo. pp. 99 (with double columns). No 59, Bleek's Catalogue of Sir George Grey's Library dealing with Australian languages, South African Public Library. Electronic file *TMs-Kaurna_to_English* provided to Rob Amery by Jane Simpson.

Teichelmann, C G, & C W Schürmann, 1840, *Outlines of a grammar, vocabulary and phraseology of the Aboriginal language of South Australia, spoken by the natives in and for some distance around Adelaide*. Adelaide: The Authors.

Tindale, Norman B, c 1934a, Paŋkala, South Australia, C W Schürmann 1884. Held at SA Museum. Identifier code: AA 338/7/2/8.

Tindale, Norman B, c 1934b, Paŋkala, South Australia, C W Schürmann 1884. Held at SA Museum. Identifier code: AA 338/7/2/9.

Tunbridge, Dorothy, 1988, 'Affixes of motion and direction in Adnyamathanha.' In P Austin (ed), *Complex sentence constructions in Australian languages*. Amsterdam: John Benjamins (267-283).

Tunbridge, Dorothy, 1996, *Mammals of the dreaming: an historical ethnomammology of the Flinders Ranges*. Doctoral dissertation, Australian National University, Canberra.

Tunstill, Guy (compiler), 2004, *Adnyamathanha years R to 10*. Adelaide: South Australian Department of Education and Children's Services.

www.ingramcontent.com/pod-product-compliance
Lightning Source LLC
Chambersburg PA
CBHW080024110526
44587CB00021BA/3835